72 YEARS OF ARTIFICIAL INTELLIGENCE INNOVATION (1950 - 2022)

A JOURNEY FROM TURING'S VISION TO CHATGPT

MOHAMMED YOUSEF SHAIK

To the visionary pioneers of Artificial Intelligence and to all those who have propelled its journey over the past 72 years, laying the foundation of a field that is reshaping our world.

To the dedicated researchers, innovators, workforce, and businesses continuously pushing the boundaries—making AI systems smarter, safer, and more impactful every day. Through their efforts, AI has evolved to possess diverse capabilities, from creativity and analytical thinking to problem-solving and adaptability, transforming industries and empowering humanity.

And to the aspiring thinkers, creators, and enterprises who will forge the next chapters in the evolution of AI.

This book is for you.

Contents

Foreword   *vii*

  1. Introduction   1

  2. 1950s: Computer Technology   4

  3. 1950-1960: Alan Turing And World War II   10

  4. 1956: Dartmouth And The Birth Of AI   15

  5. 1970s: The First AI Winter   20

  6. 1980s: The Rise Of Expert Systems   26

  7. 1986: The Introduction Of Neural Networks   31

  8. 1987-1995: The Second AI Winter   36

  9. 1997: Super Computer Defeats A Chess Grandmaster   43

10. 2000s: Machine Learning And The Rise Of Data   48

11. 2010s: The Rise Of Deep Learning   59

12. 2010s: The Rise Of Natural Language Processing (NLP)   64

13. 2010-2022: Tech Giants Driving AI Evolution   71

14. 2010-2022: AI Startups Revolution   82

15. 2010-2022: The Unnoticed AI   91

16. 2022: The Rise Of ChatGPT And LLM's   102

Understanding - AI vs Generative AI   107

Understanding AI Risks   109

AI Governance   111

Technology-Focused AI Businesses   113

Summary   115

Conclusion   123

Author Note   125

Foreword

Although AI gained significant attention with the release of ChatGPT in 2022, not much is spoken about the 72 years of innovation that led to this point. Artificial Intelligence has come a long way since its beginnings in the mid-20th century. It started with Alan Turing's seminal question, "Can machines think?" and was later formalized by John McCarthy, who coined the term "Artificial Intelligence" in 1956. Since then, AI has evolved into a vast field influencing nearly every aspect of modern life. Over the decades, breakthroughs such as expert systems, machine learning, and neural networks have transformed AI from theoretical concepts into practical applications seamlessly integrated into our daily routines

With over 18 years of experience in the IT industry, the author has designed this book to cater to busy readers, incorporating infographics, images, and bullet points for an engaging and easy-to-digest reading experience. This book is ideal for IT professionals, entrepreneurs, students, and AI enthusiasts alike. The format is carefully crafted to provide clear and concise insights on each topic, as it explores the remarkable evolution of AI.

72 years of AI Innovation (1950-2022) takes readers on a journey through the rich history of Artificial Intelligence, tracing its development from foundational milestones to its quiet integration into everyday life. This book captures the pivotal breakthroughs and technological advancements that shaped AI, from the early theories and experiments to landmark achievements in machine learning and deep learning. Alongside these milestones, it also explores the surprising ways AI has woven itself into our daily routines—through virtual assistants, recommendation systems, public safety, and more—often so seamlessly that we may not even realize the sophisticated AI behind them.

CHAPTER ONE

INTRODUCTION

Why AI Matters More Than Ever

Artificial Intelligence (AI) has evolved from a concept of science fiction to a transformative force that touches nearly every part of our lives. Today, AI influences how we communicate, shop, work, and even entertain ourselves. From the virtual assistants in our homes to the recommendation systems on social media, AI quietly shapes modern life in ways we often don't notice. For those in business, technology, or simply curious about innovation, understanding AI's journey provides insight into one of the most powerful technological evolutions of our time.

Seventy Two Years of AI Innovation (1950-2022) traces this journey from AI's early theories to its role in our daily routines. Through key milestones, we'll explore the evolution of AI, revealing both the breakthroughs and the challenges that shaped the field. This book is designed to be approachable, featuring infographics, images, and concise explanations for readers who want a clear and engaging look at how AI has evolved over the years.

AI's Journey to Necessity

2022 Beyond - Gen AI Tools

Generative AI tools like ChatGPT became integral to work and personal life.

2018 - Smart Compose

Google's Smart Compose made AI essential for professional communication.

2016 - Facebook Facial Recognition

Facebook's facial recognition improved social connectivity, integrating AI into social interactions.

2015 - Google Photos Revolution

Google Photos used AI for photo management, highlighting its necessity in organizing memories.

2015 - Alexa's Home Control

Alexa brought AI into homes, making it an accessible tool for convenience.

2011 - iPhone 4S - Siri

Siri's introduction as a voice-activated assistant marked the beginning of AI's integration into daily life.

A Journey Through AI's History

The story of AI began in the mid-20th century, sparked by the question, "Can machines think?" Visionaries like Alan Turing and John McCarthy saw potential for machines to replicate human thought, and with that came the birth of AI as a field of study. Over the decades, AI experienced phases of intense research and development, as well as setbacks known as "AI Winters," where funding and interest dwindled. Each period of resurgence brought new innovations, from expert systems in the 1980s to machine learning and deep learning advancements in the 2000s and 2010s.

This book captures these key moments, explaining how AI evolved through cycles of excitement and challenge. With a focus on major advancements like IBM's Deep Blue defeating a world chess champion and AlphaGo's victory in the game of Go, we see how AI's capabilities expanded, paving the way for applications that impact us daily.

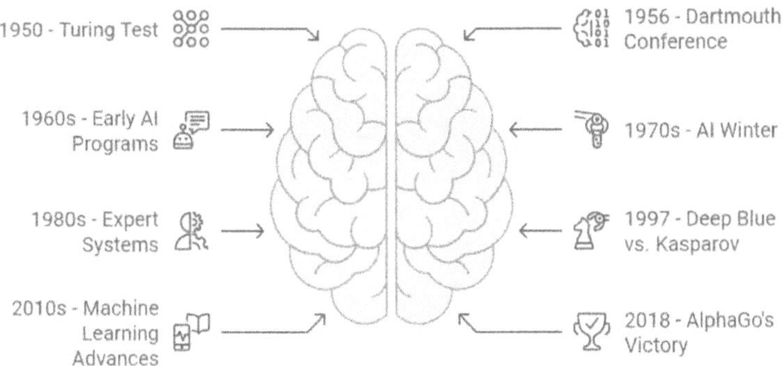

CHAPTER TWO

1950s: Computer Technology

Let's start with a brief history. We all know the concept of the computer was pioneered by Charles Babbage in the early 19th century, with his invention of the Analytical Engine in 1837. However, this was not a real computer as we know it today but rather a sophisticated mechanical calculator designed to perform basic arithmetic and algorithmic functions. The true evolution of modern computers began with the development of electronic computers in the mid-20th century.

The first generation of computers in the 1950s marked the beginning of the digital computing era. These computers, such as the UNIVAC I and IBM 701, were massive machines that filled entire rooms and used vacuum tubes for processing and storage. Although primitive by today's standards, these early computers could perform thousands of calculations per second, which was revolutionary at the time. These machines laid the groundwork for the rapid evolution of computing technology in the decades that followed.

AI representation of a 1950s computer

Size and Structure:

- 1950s computers were massive, room-sized machines that required specialized cooling systems to prevent overheating.
- These computers used large racks filled with vacuum tubes, making them bulky and power-hungry.

Main Components:

- **Vacuum Tubes:** Used as switches and amplifiers, vacuum tubes were the primary component for processing, though they generated a lot of heat and had limited reliability.
- **Magnetic Drums:** Early computers used magnetic drum memory, which had rotating cylinders coated with a magnetic material to store data.
- **Punch Cards and Paper Tape:** Data and programs were often fed into the computers using punch cards or paper tape, as there were no integrated displays or keyboards.
- **Magnetic Core Memory:** In the late 1950s, magnetic core memory began replacing drum memory as a faster and more reliable storage method.

AI Representation of Input and Output Devices

- Teletypes and Line Printers: These were used for input/output
- Oscilloscopes: Sometimes used to monitor operations

Software

Programming Languages:

- Machine Language: Computers were programmed directly in binary or machine code.
- Assembly Language: As programming evolved, assembly language was developed to make it easier to work with machine code.
- FORTRAN (1957): The first high-level programming language, FORTRAN (Formula Translation), was introduced toward the end of the 1950s, primarily for scientific and engineering applications.

Operating Systems:

- There were no full-fledged operating systems. Programs were loaded individually, run to completion, and then unloaded.
- Jobs were often batched in sequences, requiring physical intervention to load the next set of punch cards.

Applications:

- Early software focused on mathematical calculations, cryptography (such as code-breaking), scientific calculations, and military applications.
- Common applications included ballistic calculations, census data processing, and scientific research.

Computing Capabilities

Speed and Processing Power:

- Processing speeds were extremely slow by today's standards. The early computers could perform only a few thousand operations per second (measured in kilo-instructions per second or KIPS).
- For example, the UNIVAC I (one of the first commercial computers) could execute around 1,000 calculations per second.

Reliability:

- Vacuum tubes were prone to frequent failures, making computers unreliable and requiring constant maintenance.
- Machines needed regular repairs and recalibrations to function properly.

Problem-Solving Focus:

- The limited capabilities meant these computers could handle only specific tasks, mainly arithmetic and logical operations.
- They were typically used in scientific research, military calculations, cryptography, and complex engineering tasks, where repetitive calculations were needed.

Memory and Storage:

- Storage was costly and unreliable; as a result, most programs and data were stored externally on punch cards, paper tape, or magnetic drums.

Networking and Communication:

- There was no concept of networking or computer communication. Each computer operated in isolation, without any connection to other systems.

Notable Computers of the 1950s:

- **UNIVAC I (1951):** The first commercially available computer, used for business and government applications.
- **IBM 701 (1952):** IBM's first commercial scientific computer, mainly used by government agencies.
- **IBM 650 (1954):** Widely used for business applications, with magnetic drum storage.
- **Whirlwind (1951):** The first computer capable of real-time processing, used in early air defense systems.
- **Manchester Mark I, EDVAC, and LEO I:** Other significant computers used in various research and commercial applications.

These early computers laid the groundwork for modern computing, despite their limitations . They were groundbreaking for their time, representing significant advances in technology and setting the stage for future developments

CHAPTER THREE

1950-1960: Alan Turing And World War II

The Big Question: Can Machines Think?

Imagine it's 1950. The world is recovering from the devastation of World War II, and science is entering an exciting new age. In this setting, one man, Alan Turing, dares to ask a question that would shape the future: Can machines think?

Alan Turing, a brilliant British mathematician, had already helped his country by cracking enemy codes during the war. Now, he was turning his mind to something different—a vision of machines that could think and communicate like humans. In 1950, he wrote a paper called "Computing Machinery and Intelligence," where he introduced a simple yet bold test to answer his question.

TURING TEST

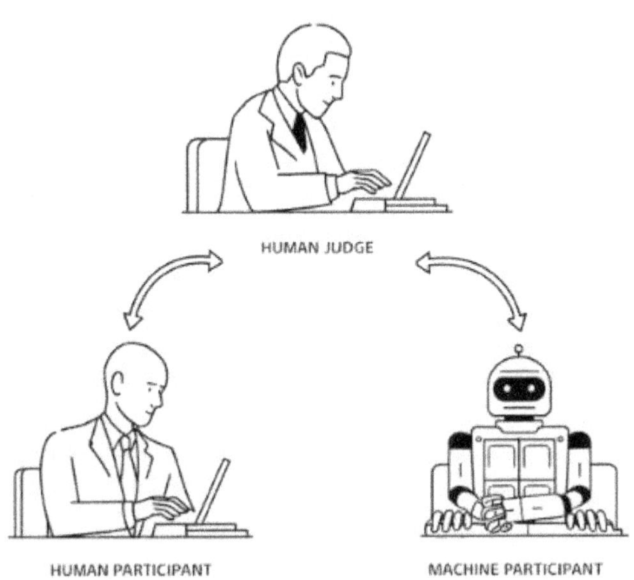

In this test, which we now call the Turing Test, a human judge communicates with two hidden participants—one human and one machine. If the judge can't tell which is which, Turing argued, then maybe the machine could be considered "intelligent." The Turing Test was a big idea, and it raised a new question: Could a machine ever act just like a person?

The Turing Test didn't take place in the 1950s because the technology simply wasn't advanced enough. Computers at the time lacked the processing power, memory, and programming sophistication required to simulate human conversation convincingly. AI was still in its infancy, and creating a machine capable of mimicking human intelligence was far beyond the capabilities of early computers. Turing's idea served as a visionary goal for the future, rather than an immediate experiment.

The Universal Turing Machine: A New Kind of Machine

Before he proposed the Turing Test, Alan Turing had another big idea in 1936. He imagined a machine that could be programmed to solve any problem, not just one specific task. This idea was called the Universal Turing Machine, and it became the foundation for modern computers.

Turing's vision was simple but powerful: if a machine could be programmed, then it could be taught to perform many tasks—not just calculations, but logical steps to reach a solution.This universal machine was like a blank canvas, ready to be shaped by different programs to accomplish any goal. It was the first step toward computers that could learn and adapt, opening up new possibilities for what machines could do.

Turing's ideas inspired scientists to think of machines in a whole new way. If a machine could be programmed to follow logical steps, just like a person thinks through a problem, then maybe it could "learn" and make decisions. Turing believed that machines could be more than calculators; they could be thinkers.

Although Turing's ideas were groundbreaking, not everyone was ready to believe in the potential of thinking machines. The 1950s and '60s saw a mix of excitement and doubt as scientists tried to explore the possibilities Turing had opened up.Yet his work left a lasting legacy, inspiring generations of researchers.

Turing's ideas continue to influence AI today. Every time we interact with a virtual assistant or see a recommendation on social media, we're experiencing the effects of his visionary work. The Turing Test and the concept of a universal machine are still central ideas in AI, reminding us of the big question that started it all: Can machines really think?

AI representation of World War II

Alan Turing's contributions in World War II

During World War II, Alan Turing played a pivotal role in cryptography at Bletchley Park, the British government's code-breaking center. His work focused on cracking the Enigma code, an encryption system used by Nazi Germany to send military messages. The Enigma machine had a complex and changeable encryption process, making German communications virtually unbreakable—until Turing's groundbreaking work.

Breaking the Enigma Code:

- Turing developed techniques to decipher Enigma-encrypted messages, which changed settings daily to create millions of possible configurations.

- His mathematical insights enabled him to identify patterns and develop strategies to decode the messages, giving the Allies a strategic advantage.

The Bombe Machine:

- To speed up the code-breaking process, Turing helped design a machine called the Bombe. The Bombe was an electromechanical device that tested multiple Enigma settings quickly, narrowing down the correct configuration.
- Turing's machine could analyze intercepted Enigma messages in hours, drastically improving the speed and effectiveness of decoding German messages.

Impact on the War:

- Turing's work allowed the Allies to anticipate German military plans, from troop movements to submarine attacks.
- Historians estimate that his work at Bletchley Park shortened the war by as much as two years and saved countless lives.

Turing's code-breaking work not only helped win the war but also laid the foundation for modern computing, as his approach to solving the Enigma puzzle was an early application of what we now consider algorithmic thinking.

CHAPTER FOUR

1956: DARTMOUTH AND THE BIRTH OF AI

In the summer of 1956, a small group of visionary scientists gathered at Dartmouth College in New Hampshire with one goal: to explore the idea that machines could be made to "think." This historic meeting would later be known as the Dartmouth Conference, and it marked the official birth of the field we now call Artificial Intelligence (AI).

At the center of this gathering was **John McCarthy**, a young computer scientist who believed that machines could replicate human intelligence. It was McCarthy who coined the term **"Artificial Intelligence"** to capture the ambition of creating machines capable of performing tasks that, until then, were thought to require human intelligence. His choice of words was deliberate, meant to convey the idea of not just mechanical calculation but of genuine "thinking" machines.

AI representation of Dartmouth Conference - 1956

The Visionary Goals of the Dartmouth Conference

The Dartmouth Conference was more than just a meeting; it was a leap into the unknown. McCarthy and his colleagues, including Marvin Minsky, Nathaniel Rochester, and Claude Shannon, put forward bold ideas that would set the direction for AI research for decades. They believed that intelligence—perception, language, reasoning—could be recreated in a machine

The group laid out ambitious goals:

- **To simulate human thought:** They aimed to understand and replicate processes like reasoning, problem-solving, and learning within a machine.
- **To create machines that could learn:** The concept of machine learning was still in its infancy, but they dreamed of machines that could adapt and improve without human intervention.
- **To push the boundaries of computer science:** This wasn't just about building smarter machines; it was about pioneering a new field of study. They wanted to combine mathematics, logic, engineering, and psychology to give birth to something entirely new.

To push the boundaries of computer science: This wasn't just about building smarter machines; it was about pioneering a new field of study. They wanted to combine mathematics, logic, engineering, and psychology to give birth to something entirely new.

The conference attendees knew they were only scratching the surface, but they saw AI as a way to unlock new possibilities for technology and humanity.

The legacy of the Dartmouth Conference lies not only in the scientific goals it set but also in its spirit of collaboration and exploration. It marked the formal beginning of AI as a field of study, inspiring generations of researchers to pursue the dream of intelligent machines. The attendees left Dartmouth with more questions than answers, yet united in their commitment to uncover the potential of machines— a commitment that propelled AI research forward through both triumphs and setbacks.

The Dartmouth Conference Participants and Their Lasting Impact on AI

The participants of the Dartmouth Conference left with a shared vision that machines could simulate aspects of human intelligence, sparking a lifelong commitment to advancing AI. They each went on to pioneer new ideas—John McCarthy developed the Lisp programming language, Marvin Minsky advanced robotics and neural networks, and Nathaniel Rochester contributed to early AI programming techniques

John McCarthy : Developed the Lisp programming language, essential for AI programming, and worked extensively on concepts like time-sharing and commonsense reasoning.

Marvin Minsky : He was a pioneer in machine perception, robotics, and neural networks. He co-founded the <u>MIT Artificial Intelligence Laboratory</u> and made significant contributions to the understanding of machine learning and the structure of intelligence. Minsky also authored influential books on AI, such as Perceptrons (with Seymour Papert) and The Society of Mind.

Nathaniel Rochester: He was IBM scientist and expert in computer hardware, ochester helped create the first assembler (an early programming language) and was involved in the development of IBM's 701 computer. Rochester's expertise in computing hardware was crucial in exploring the feasibility of building intelligent machines.

Claude Shannon: Also known as father of information theory. Shannon laid the groundwork for modern digital circuit design theory and information theory. His work on Boolean logic and communication theory provided a theoretical foundation for data processing, which is essential to AI. Shannon was interested in the idea of teaching machines to learn and problem-solve.

More About John McCarthy: Father of Artificial Intelligence

He developed Lisp Programming Language (1958), one of the earliest programming languages designed specifically for AI research. Lisp became the primary language for AI programming for many years due to its flexibility and ability to handle symbolic reasoning, an essential feature for AI applications.Lisp introduced concepts like recursive functions and automatic memory management, which influenced many modern programming languages

McCarthy was instrumental in pioneering the concept of time-sharing in computing, which allowed multiple users to share a single computer's resources simultaneously. This innovation made computing more accessible and efficient, laying the foundation for modern multi-user and networked systems.

McCarthy believed that true AI would require the ability to understand and reason about everyday situations. He introduced the idea of commonsense reasoning in AI, which is the ability of machines to make logical inferences about the world, much like humans do.

McCarthy received numerous awards for his contributions, including the Turing Award in 1971, which is often regarded as the "Nobel Prize of Computing"

Other Notable Contributors

Though not present at Dartmouth, scientists like **Allen Newell** and **Herbert A. Simon** (who later developed the Logic Theorist, one of the first AI programs) were contemporaries whose work paralleled the ideas explored at the Dartmouth Conference.

CHAPTER FIVE

1970s: The First AI Winter

The First AI Winter

As the excitement and optimism from the early days of artificial intelligence began to grow, so did the challenges. By the 1970s, AI faced its first major setback, a period now referred to as the "AI Winter." This decade saw a significant drop in enthusiasm, funding, and progress in the field of AI. Despite the initial breakthroughs and ambitious goals set during the Dartmouth Conference in 1956, reality began to set in—AI was proving to be a much harder problem than anyone had anticipated.

The early promises of AI fueled high expectations, with governments and institutions investing heavily, hoping for breakthroughs. However, researchers soon encountered unexpected challenges as systems struggled with tasks humans found simple, widening the gap between ambition and reality. This growing frustration led to skepticism and a gradual cooling of support.

AI representation of stalled projects

The Root Causes of the AI Winter

Several factors contributed to this downturn in AI research. Key among them were:

- **Technical Limitations:** The hardware of the time was simply not capable of supporting the complex computations required for advanced AI. Computers were slow, expensive, and lacked sufficient memory. Tasks like natural language processing and pattern recognition, which seemed achievable in theory, required far more computational power than was available.
- **Overpromised Goals:** Early researchers in AI made bold claims, suggesting that machines could quickly achieve human-like intelligence. These claims were often picked up by the media and fueled public expectation. When these ambitious predictions failed to materialize, it led to disappointment and skepticism among both the public and the scientific community.

- **Competition from Other Technologies:** During the 1970s, other areas of technology were advancing rapidly. Fields like software engineering, data processing, and general computer science offered more immediate benefits, drawing talent and resources away from AI research. These technologies were not only more feasible but also provided quicker returns on investment.

The Impact of the AI Winter

- **Reduced Research Activity:** With little funding and support, AI research was scaled back drastically. Many researchers shifted their focus to other fields, while AI departments were downsized or closed in various academic institutions.
- **Negative Perception:** The public and media began to view AI as overhyped and unrealistic. This negative perception further discouraged funding agencies, creating a vicious cycle of declining support and innovation.

The AI Winter of the 1970s, while difficult, provided important lessons that would shape the future of artificial intelligence. Researchers learned the importance of setting realistic goals and aligning expectations with technological feasibility. As funding dwindled, the field began to redefine itself, moving away from the promise of human-level intelligence to focus on more achievable, task-specific AI applications.

The lessons learned during this period encouraged researchers to adopt a more pragmatic approach, focusing on solving specific problems rather than pursuing the broader, elusive goal of general intelligence.

AI Projects That Fell Short of Expectations

Expectation-Driven Robotics Projects : Late 1960's

Aim: These robotics projects aimed to develop autonomous robots capable of performing complex, human-like tasks in real-world environments. The goal was for robots to navigate, make decisions, and interact with objects based on expected outcomes, potentially assisting in industrial and domestic tasks.

Challenges and Outcomes: The primary hurdle was the limited capability of early sensors and control systems, which lacked the precision needed for tasks requiring dexterity and adaptability. Furthermore, the expectation-driven models relied on assumptions about predictable environments; they struggled with unexpected changes, making the robots unreliable in dynamic or unfamiliar settings. As a result, the robots were restricted to simple, repetitive actions in controlled conditions, falling short of the initial vision of fully autonomous, adaptive robotics.

AI representation of Robotics

Speech Understanding Research (SUR) Program : Early 1970's

Aim: The goal of the Speech Understanding Research (SUR) program was to create a system capable of understanding continuous, naturally spoken language. The program aimed for a system that could recognize a large vocabulary and respond accurately to spoken commands, paving the way for more interactive human-computer communication.

Challenges and Outcomes: The system struggled with natural speech variations in tone, speed, and accent. Limited processing power made real-time recognition nearly impossible, while inflexible algorithms led to frequent errors. As a result, it was restricted to controlled environments with predefined vocabularies, falling short of its goal to understand natural, free-flowing speech.

AI representation of Speech Understanding System

Early Machine Translation Program : Early 1960's

Aim: The goal of early machine translation programs was to develop systems capable of translating foreign texts accurately and reliably, particularly in areas requiring quick communication. These systems aimed to handle complex sentences and varied linguistic structures, breaking language barriers.

Challenges and Outcomes: These systems faced major hurdles in understanding context, syntax, and idiomatic expressions. Early algorithms often produced translations that were technically correct but missed the intended meaning. Limited processing power restricted real-time translation and adaptation to linguistic variations, and a critical review in the mid-1960s found the technology impractical and costly, leading to reduced funding and slowed development.

AI representation of Machine Translation Program

CHAPTER SIX

1980s: The Rise Of Expert Systems

After the setbacks of the 1970s, The 1980s saw a resurgence of interest in AI, driven largely by the development and success of software based "expert systems." These programs, designed to mimic the decision-making abilities of human experts, marked a significant shift in the application of AI, with a focus on solving real-world problems in specific industries. Expert systems rekindled excitement and funding for AI, showing that while creating a truly intelligent machine might still be out of reach, computers could excel within narrow domains.

Expert systems are computer programs that emulate the reasoning and decision-making processes of a human expert in a particular field. Unlike general AI, which aims for broad intelligence, expert systems focus on specialized knowledge. They use a combination of rules, knowledge bases, and inference engines to analyze data and provide insights, diagnoses, or recommendations, simulating the thought processes of experts in areas like medicine, finance, and engineering.

AI representation of Expert System in 1980's

The expert systems of the 1980s were primarily software-based programs, designed to run on standard computer hardware of the time, rather than requiring specialized hardware, some of hardware include

- **Mainframes and Minicomputers:** Many expert systems were developed to run on powerful mainframes or minicomputers rather than personal computers, due to their intensive processing needs. IBM mainframes and DEC (Digital Equipment Corporation) minicomputers, such as the VAX series.

- **Workstations:** Some expert systems ran on advanced workstations designed for scientific and engineering applications, such as those produced by companies like Symbolics, Texas Instruments, and Xerox. These workstations were optimized for AI applications and symbolic processing.
- **Personal Computers:** By the late 1980s, with the increasing power of personal computers, some simpler expert systems could run on personal computers with adequate memory and processing speed, though they were limited in capabilities compared to those on mainframes.

Well-known examples of expert systems from the 1980s

- **MYCIN (Healthcare):** Developed at Stanford University, MYCIN was designed to diagnose bacterial infections and recommend treatments based on symptoms and patient data.
- **DENDRAL (Chemistry/Biochemistry):** Created in the 1960s and refined in the 1970s and 1980s, DENDRAL was one of the first expert systems and was used to assist chemists in determining molecular structures. DENDRAL proved that expert systems could perform specialized scientific tasks as well as, or sometimes better than, human experts.
- **PROSPECTOR (Geology/Mining):** Was developed to help geologists identify potential mineral deposits. It famously helped locate a valuable molybdenum deposit in Washington State, demonstrating its effectiveness in the field.
- **DELTA (Airline Operations):** This expert system assisted in scheduling and routing decisions, optimizing flight operations and crew assignments. DELTA showed the value of expert systems in operations and logistics, proving that AI could solve complex scheduling issues in real-time.

- **XCON (R1):** Developed by DEC (Digital Equipment Corporation) for use on their own VAX minicomputers, XCON was both a software application and a showcase of DEC's hardware capabilities. DEC's VAX series minicomputers were powerful machines designed to support complex computing needs, and XCON was optimized to run on DEC's own systems, benefiting from their hardware's robustness and processing capabilities.
- **CATS (Computer-Aided Troubleshooting System) for Aircraft Maintenance:** CATS was developed to assist aircraft maintenance teams in diagnosing mechanical issues and ensuring safe, efficient repairs.The system used fault diagnosis rules and maintenance records to identify probable causes of mechanical problems, guiding technicians through troubleshooting steps.CATS improved the speed and accuracy of aircraft maintenance, reducing downtime and enhancing safety. It showed the utility of expert systems in sectors where reliability and safety are paramount.

Software and Programming Languages

- **LISP and Prolog:** Many expert systems were written in LISP and Prolog, languages well-suited to symbolic processing, which is essential for rule-based reasoning. LISP machines by Symbolics and Texas Instruments were designed specifically to optimize LISP performance, providing a significant boost for AI applications.
- **Shells and Frameworks:** In the late 1980s, expert system shells (software frameworks for building expert systems) became available for personal computers, allowing simpler systems to be developed on PCs. Some popular expert system shells were CLIPS (developed by NASA) and OPS5.

People Behind the Innovation:

- **Edward Feigenbaum:** known as the "father of expert systems," played a crucial role in developing early systems like DENDRAL, which helped chemists analyze molecular structures.
- **Randall Davis:** contributed to the MYCIN expert system for diagnosing bacterial infections, which demonstrated the potential of AI in healthcare.
- **John McDermott:** McDermott developed R1, also known as XCON (eXpert CONfigurer) for the Digital Equipment Corporation (DEC).
- **Carla Gomes:** Her research focused on expanding the problem-solving capabilities of expert systems and making them more adaptable.
- **Patrick Winston:** A professor at MIT and one of the early leaders in artificial intelligence, Winston contributed to knowledge representation and the development of expert systems.
- **Peter Friedland:** Friedland played a significant role in expanding expert systems into different fields. As a key contributor to DENDRAL and later projects, he helped bring expert systems technology to applications outside of chemistry, including space exploration at NASA.

Some expert systems, like XCON, saw significant commercial success and return on investment. Despite their usefulness, expert systems were expensive to maintain and update. The systems required teams of knowledge engineers to continually refine the rules and input new knowledge. This high maintenance cost was a factor in the eventual decline of expert systems when more flexible machine learning approaches, like neural networks, emerged.

CHAPTER SEVEN

1986: THE INTRODUCTION OF NEURAL NETWORKS

Neural networks were not a new concept; they originated with Warren McCulloch and Walter Pitts in the 1940s, inspired by biological neurons and the way the human brain processes information. However, initial excitement around these networks faded by the 1970s due to technological limitations. Early neural networks, such as Frank Rosenblatt's Perceptron, could only handle basic tasks and struggled with more complex ones due to limited processing power and unsophisticated algorithms.

The key breakthrough in 1986 regarding backpropagation was primarily developed and popularized by David E. Rumelhart, Geoffrey Hinton, and Ronald J. Williams. Their work on backpropagation, especially through the influential paper "Learning representations by back-propagating errors," reintroduced and refined the concept, making it a practical and powerful method for training neural networks. This development helped rekindle interest in neural networks and laid the foundation for modern deep learning techniques.

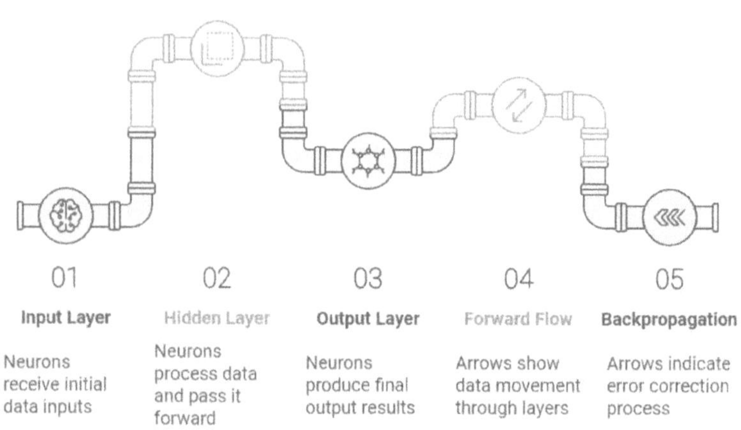

Backpropagation was not just a theoretical concept; it was practically proven and implemented.

Handwriting Recognition

- **Task:** The neural network was trained to recognize handwritten characters. This task involved analyzing pixel patterns in the images of characters and identifying the correct letter or digit
- **Backpropagation's Role:** By adjusting weights across multiple layers in response to errors, backpropagation enabled the network to gradually improve its accuracy in recognizing characters, even in the presence of variations in handwriting styles.
- **Outcome:** The success in recognizing handwritten characters showed that backpropagation could effectively enable a network to learn complex, non-linear mappings, which was a significant improvement over single-layer networks.

Image Classification (Simple Objects)

- **Task:** In another use case, backpropagation was applied to classify simple images based on patterns. For instance, the network might learn to distinguish between different shapes or patterns within a limited dataset.
- **Backpropagation's Role:** The algorithm allowed the network to adjust its weights by processing errors from the output layer back to the hidden layers, fine-tuning the model to make better predictions with each iteration.
- **Outcome:** This demonstrated that multi-layered networks could identify intricate patterns and classify images, laying the groundwork for more advanced computer vision applications.

Speech Recognition (Preliminary Experiments)

- Task: Early experiments also applied backpropagation to simple speech recognition tasks, where the network would process audio signals to recognize phonemes or words.
- Backpropagation's Role: The algorithm helped the network learn to associate patterns in sound frequencies with specific phonemes, allowing it to improve over time.
- Outcome: While limited by the technology of the time, these experiments showed the potential of backpropagation for speech processing, a field that would later become critical in AI.

Why These Tasks Were Chosen

These tasks—handwriting recognition, image classification, and preliminary speech recognition—were chosen because they are classic pattern recognition problems, which backpropagation is well-suited to solve. These early use cases proved that backpropagation enabled networks to learn complex patterns and adapt based on errors, moving neural networks beyond simple linear models

AI Model Used - Multilayer Perceptron (MLP)

The MLP, while not the first AI model, represented a major advancement in neural networks and machine learning. Geoffrey Hinton, David Rumelhart, and Ronald J. Williams were instrumental in its development through their work on backpropagation. They programmed their models using languages like FORTRAN, LISP, and C

Data Preparation: Converting Images for Neural Network Training

- **Digitization of Images:** The handwritten digits were scanned and digitized. Each image was transformed into a pixel grid, each pixel in the grid was represented by a grayscale value
- **Flattening the Image:** Each pixel's grayscale value became an individual input value in this vector. So, an image of a digit would be represented by 784 numerical values when fed into the network.
- **Batching and Normalization:**To improve training efficiency, images were grouped into batches and processed in sets during each training step. Batch processing made calculations more efficient and helped stabilize the training process.
- **Labeling:** Each image was associated with a label indicating the correct digit (0–9) in the training dataset. This label served as the "ground truth" for calculating error during training.

The Transition to Data-Driven AI

As neural networks began to show promise in recognizing patterns and learning from data, AI researchers started to realize that algorithms alone weren't enough; the true potential of these systems would only be unlocked by feeding them vast amounts of data. Where large datasets fuel the learning process. While neural networks allowed machines to adjust based on input. This marked a shift toward what we now call "**Data-driven AI**,"

AI representation of large-scale data input

The exploration of neural networks in the 1980s and 1990s helped shape the approach to machine learning that would become central in the 2000s. Neural networks introduced the concept of learning from data, paving the way for machine learning algorithms designed to identify patterns, predict outcomes, and adapt to new information. Unlike traditional programming, where rules were explicitly coded, machine learning allowed systems to improve by finding patterns within data—a concept rooted in the early work on neural networks.

CHAPTER EIGHT

1987-1995: THE SECOND AI WINTER

Optimism in AI revived in the 1980s, fueled by the success of expert systems and new funding initiatives focused on advancing computing technology. However, as these ambitious projects encountered technical and practical limitations, enthusiasm began to cool once more. Between 1987 and 1995, a series of setbacks contributed to what would come to be known as the Second AI Winter.

The Second AI Winter was marked by diminishing confidence in AI's ability to deliver on its promises. As projects faced challenges in processing power, limited algorithms, and constrained memory. Researchers encountered difficulties in scaling AI beyond narrow domains, leading to frustrations among investors and decision-makers.

Research labs faced budget cuts, and many AI projects were either slowed, put on hold, or canceled due to unmet expectations and technological limitations. Institutions and investors became increasingly cautious, redirecting funds to areas with more immediate returns, such as traditional computing and software development

Key Instances and Events

1987: The Collapse of the Lisp Machine Market

- **Background:** Lisp machines, were specialized computers for AI programming, particularly for running expert systems and symbolic processing tasks.
- **Event:** By 1987, personal computers had become much more powerful, affordable, and versatile. General-purpose hardware, such as PCs with increased memory and processing speeds, began to overshadow Lisp machines. Companies could no longer justify the high cost of maintaining dedicated Lisp machines, leading to a rapid collapse of the market.
- **Impact:** The collapse of the Lisp machine market marked a shift away from specialized AI hardware. This event symbolized a broader disillusionment in AI as companies and investors questioned the viability of expensive, specialized AI technology.

AI representation of LISP machine

1988: Defense Agency Shift in Priorities for AI Research

- **Background:** The Defense Research Agency was a major funder of AI research, supporting ambitious applications in defense, such as automated planning, speech recognition, and robotics.
- **Event:** Following underwhelming results from its Strategic Computing Initiative—which aimed to develop AI-powered military applications—the agency scaled back its AI investments and redirected funds toward other priorities, such as missile defense and information security.
- **Impact:** The agency's decision to reduce AI funding left many research projects underfunded or canceled. This shift created a significant funding gap, particularly in the fields of natural language processing and robotics, which impacted both academic and commercial AI development.

AI representation of defence AI research center

1991: AI's Commercial Struggles in the Financial Sector

- **Background:** AI applications in finance, such as automated trading systems and risk assessment models, had been a focal point for investment in the late 1980s. Financial institutions hoped AI could provide insights and automation to give them a competitive edge.
- **Event:** By the early 1990s, several AI-driven financial systems underperformed. These systems often failed to adapt to rapidly changing market conditions, leading to poor ROI.
- **Impact:** High-profile failures in financial AI applications contributed to a loss of confidence in AI's practical value. Financial institutions became more cautious about investing in experimental AI, shifting instead to data analytics and traditional algorithmic models.

AI representation of commercial struggles

1992: Decline of Interest in Expert Systems

- **Background:** Expert systems, which dominated AI applications in the 1980s, were designed to simulate human expertise in specific fields through rule-based programming.
- **Event:** By 1992, many expert systems had been discontinued or scaled back as they proved difficult and costly to maintain. Updating these systems required continuous input from human experts, and their rule-based logic often made them inflexible and error-prone.
- **Impact:** The limitations of expert systems underscored the need for AI approaches that could adapt and learn from data, rather than relying solely on predefined rules. This period helped shift AI research interest toward machine learning, which would later lead to the resurgence of neural networks.

AI representation of expert systems

1992: The End Japan's Fifth Generation Computer Systems (FGCS) Project

- **Background:** Launched in 1982, the FGCS project set out to develop computers capable of human-like reasoning, natural language understanding, and advanced problem-solving. This ambitious initiative was initially hailed as a potential breakthrough in AI, sparking global interest and competition.
- **Event:** Over the years, however, it became clear that FGCS was not meeting its objectives. Despite significant investment and advances in parallel processing, the project struggled in critical areas like natural language processing and logical reasoning.
- **Impact:** When the FGCS project formally ended in 1992, its limitations underscored the technological constraints of the era. The challenges faced by FGCS led other nations to approach similar large-scale AI projects with caution, highlighting the gap between AI ambitions and real-world capabilities.

AI representation of FGCS project

Lessons from the Second AI Winter

Technological Reality Check: The second AI winter highlighted the importance of aligning research goals with available technology. Ambitious AI projects failed primarily because they demanded more computational power, storage, and adaptability than the technology of the time could provide.

Rise of Pragmatic AI: As AI funding dwindled, researchers and companies shifted focus to achievable, narrow applications rather than broad AI goals. This pragmatic approach led to the exploration of machine learning models that could adapt from data rather than rely on rigid rules, a shift that would prove vital for future AI progress.

Cautious Optimism in AI Research: The lessons of the second AI winter tempered expectations around AI. Researchers and investors became more cautious about hype, favoring incremental progress over grand visions. This cautious optimism allowed AI research to rebuild its foundations on solid, evidence-based achievements.

The End of the Winter, by the mid-1990s, as computing power continued to improve and data-driven methods began to take shape, AI started to emerge from the second winter. Researchers moved beyond symbolic AI, embracing machine learning and neural networks. This shift laid the groundwork for the AI advancements of the late 1990s and early 2000s, ushering in a new era of AI powered by data, statistical models, and more realistic ambitions. The second AI winter served as a crucial period of recalibration, realigning AI's goals with technological capabilities and setting the stage for a resurgence driven by machine learning, deep learning, and, eventually, data-driven AI.

CHAPTER NINE

1997: Super Computer Defeats A Chess Grandmaster

In the mid-1990s, artificial intelligence had made inroads into many areas, but one of its most formidable challenges lay in the ancient game of chess. With its immense range of possible moves and complex strategies, chess was seen as a definitive test of human intelligence and problem-solving skill. The goal of creating a computer that could defeat a human chess grandmaster had been a long-standing ambition for AI researchers—and in 1997, this ambition was partially accomplished when IBM's Deep Blue scored a victory in a game against the reigning world champion, Garry Kasparov.

This victory was groundbreaking, marking the first time a machine had managed to defeat a world champion in a standard game under tournament conditions. Although Kasparov ultimately won the overall match, Deep Blue's success in a single game signaled that machines were edging closer to competing with human intelligence in complex, strategic tasks.

AI representation of Man vs Machine

IBM's Deep Blue Vs Garry Kasparov

In February 1997, Deep Blue faced Garry Kasparov, the reigning world chess champion and widely considered one of the greatest chess players in history. The match was structured as a standard six-game tournament, with the same rules that governed human chess championships.

1. **The First Game:** Deep Blue made history by winning the first game of the match, marking the first time a computer had defeated a reigning world champion under traditional tournament conditions. This victory sent shockwaves through the world of chess and AI, demonstrating that machines could compete at the highest levels of human cognition.

2. **Kasparov's Comeback:** Despite Deep Blue's strong start, Kasparov adapted to the machine's playing style over the next games. He won three games and drew two, ultimately winning the match with a score of 4-2.

Building a Digital Chess Master

Chess has long been recognized as a prime challenge for computers trying to match the strategic depth of human intelligence. With its countless possible moves and complex strategies, chess presents significant computational demands. The sheer volume of potential moves—around 10^{40} legal combinations, or approximately 10,000,000,000,000,000,000,000,000,000,000,000,000,000 moves—requires vast processing power for a computer to make competitive decisions.

1957: IBM engineer and mathematician Alex Bernstein created the first full-fledged computer chess program, running it on an IBM 704. This program could execute 42,000 instructions per second with a memory capacity of 70 kilobytes.

1962: At MIT, researchers developed a new program on the IBM 7090, which marked a leap forward by playing chess more credibly. It evaluated 1,100 board positions per second, bringing machine chess closer to human-like play.

1970s: By this decade, chess programs had evolved to win various amateur tournaments. However, they still fell short of achieving grandmaster-level play, highlighting the ongoing gap between machine and human strategic capabilities.

While early chess programs made impressive strides, they still fell short of matching a grandmaster's intuition and strategy. Each advancement showcased progress but underscored the limits of existing technology. The dream of a true digital chess master remained, fueling further AI innovations that would ultimately lead to breakthroughs like IBM's Deep Blue.

Building Deep Blue

Deep Blue's journey began in the 1980s with a project led by computer scientists Feng-hsiung Hsu and Murray Campbell. Initially, they developed a chess-playing machine called ChipTest, followed by an advanced version named Deep Thought, which went on to defeat a chess grandmaster. Recognizing the potential, IBM recruited Hsu and Campbell in 1989, and Deep Blue was born. The team focused on creating a machine capable of competing at the highest level of chess. Over years of research, they built a system with 32 parallel processors that could evaluate around 200 million chess positions per second—a staggering computational power at the time.

Technical Innovations: Deep Blue's architecture was designed to handle the immense complexity of chess. The machine used specialized hardware to speed up search algorithms, enabling it to process potential moves and countermoves at an unprecedented rate. One of its core strengths was its evaluation function, which incorporated rules and strategies used by grandmasters. Deep Blue was programmed to anticipate opponent moves, identify potential threats, and assess board positions with a high degree of accuracy. The team integrated an extensive database of historical games, enabling Deep Blue to "learn" from past strategies and use that knowledge to adapt during games.

Years of Development: Deep Blue's development required ongoing refinement, especially in handling strategic play beyond brute-force calculations. The team collaborated with chess experts to refine its decision-making algorithms, ensuring that the machine could handle both complex tactics and endgame scenarios. These refinements took nearly a decade of dedicated research and incremental advancements, making Deep Blue one of the most sophisticated examples of artificial intelligence at the time.

The Rematch: IBM's Deep Blue vs. Garry Kasparov

An upgraded version of Deep Blue faced Kasparov again, this time with even greater processing power and enhanced algorithms. In a historic outcome, Deep Blue won the rematch with a score of 3.5-2.5, becoming the first computer to defeat a world champion in a full match under standard tournament rules.

AI Representation of a Machine in the Spotlight

IBM's Deep Blue victory over Garry Kasparov captivated global media, making front-page news and sparking widespread public interest in artificial intelligence. This landmark event established AI as a serious field of research and innovation in the eyes of both the public and investors, inspiring curiosity about its potential across various industries. Deep Blue's success fueled debates on AI's future, with implications extending beyond chess to fields like finance and healthcare.

This pivotal moment set the foundation for the next era, where AI would evolve beyond specific tasks—driven by machine learning and fueled by vast amounts of data.

CHAPTER TEN

2000s: Machine Learning And The Rise of Data

A New Era for Artificial Intelligence

The early 2000s marked a turning point for artificial intelligence as machine learning emerged as a transformative approach, reshaping the field with new applications and capabilities. Unlike traditional rule-based systems, machine learning allowed computers to learn directly from data, adapt to new information, and make increasingly accurate predictions. This advancement enabled AI to tackle complex, real-world problems in fields like healthcare, finance, and customer service, where adaptability and data-driven insights became critical.

As machine learning continued to evolve, it laid the groundwork for AI systems that could operate autonomously, analyze trends, and refine their performance over time. These developments marked the beginning of a data-centric era, where the focus on data quality and quantity fueled unprecedented innovation across industries.

AI representation of digital connectivity and surge in data

In the early 2000s, the rapid growth of digital connectivity led to an unprecedented surge in data generation. As more people gained access to mobile phones, computers, and the internet, the amount of available data increased exponentially. This vast pool of information provided fertile ground for machine learning algorithms, which rely on large datasets to uncover patterns, make predictions, and improve accuracy over time.

The widespread adoption of smartphones and internet connectivity around the globe further accelerated data creation. From social media interactions to online shopping and sensor data from smart devices, an enormous variety of data types became accessible. This data influx not only fueled the growth of machine learning but also pushed the boundaries of what AI could achieve in understanding, processing, and predicting human behavior and market trends

This rapid increase in data transformed machine learning from a niche research area into a powerful tool with real-world applications. As data continued to grow.

The Core of Machine Learning: Learning from Data

At its foundation, machine learning is about enabling computers to improve their performance on specific tasks through experience—essentially, learning from data. This process relies on training algorithms on vast datasets, allowing systems to identify patterns, make decisions, and generate predictions. The availability of massive datasets in the 2000s provided machine learning algorithms with the raw material they needed to develop robust and adaptable models.

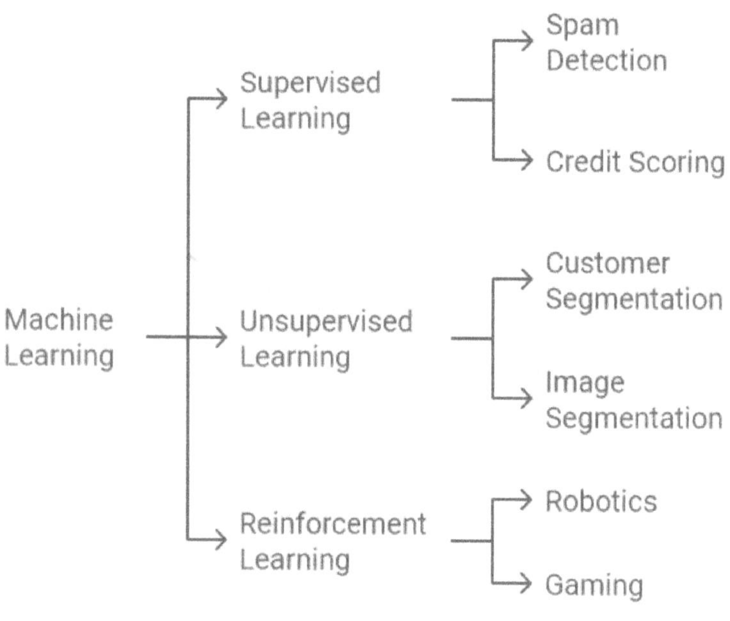

Examples

Above are few examples of real-world applications for supervised learning, unsupervised learning, and reinforcement learning, as illustrated above.

1. **Supervised Learning:** In supervised learning, systems are trained on labeled data—datasets with known outcomes—to make future predictions. Examples include spam detection in emails and credit scoring in finance.
2. **Unsupervised Learning:** In contrast, unsupervised learning uses unlabeled data to find patterns, such as grouping customers by purchasing behavior or segmenting images by similar features.
3. **Reinforcement Learning:** Although less prominent in the 2000s, reinforcement learning (where systems learn by trial and error) laid the groundwork for future applications in robotics and gaming.

Machine learning's core principles—learning from data—found fertile ground in a world of rapidly expanding digital information. With new techniques like supervised, unsupervised, and reinforcement learning, machine learning became adaptable to a range of applications, from personalized recommendations to predictive analytics in finance. The surge in available data and computational power allowed algorithms to evolve from static models into dynamic systems. This era laid the foundation for future breakthroughs, pushing AI beyond theoretical research and into practical, real-world implementations.

The evolution of machine learning techniques also paved the way for hybrid approaches that combine supervised, unsupervised, and reinforcement learning methods to address more complex problems. For example, semi-supervised learning, which leverages both labeled and unlabeled data, emerged as a critical tool in scenarios where fully labeled datasets are scarce or expensive to create. Similarly, deep reinforcement learning integrated neural networks into reinforcement learning, enabling breakthroughs in areas like autonomous driving and advanced robotics.

The Role of Big Data in Machine Learning's Rise

The rise of big data was critical to machine learning's evolution. As internet usage skyrocketed, enormous amounts of information became available from sources like search engines, social media, e-commerce, and IoT devices. Companies began to recognize the immense value embedded in this data and invested heavily in storing and analyzing it.

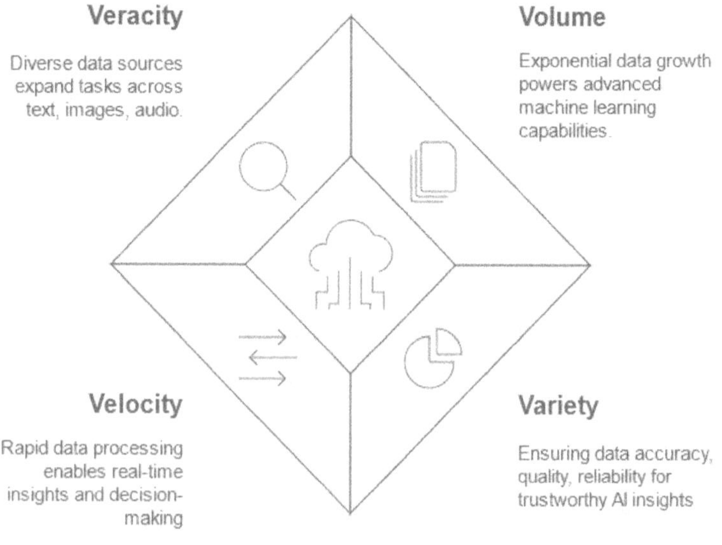

Understanding The Foundational Attributes

- **Volume:** The sheer scale of data grew exponentially, creating vast opportunities for training more powerful machine learning models. Google and Amazon were among the early pioneers in leveraging massive datasets to improve their search algorithms and recommendation systems.

- **Variety:** Data sources became diverse, with information coming from text, images, audio, and video. This variety expanded the types of tasks machine learning could handle, from image recognition to natural language processing.
- **Velocity:** Data was generated and processed faster than ever, allowing real-time analysis. This capability was critical for applications like stock trading, where machine learning models needed to react quickly to market fluctuations.
- **Veracity:** As data volumes grew, ensuring data quality, accuracy, and reliability became crucial. Machine learning models are only as good as the data they're trained on, so addressing issues like data noise, inconsistencies, and biases became essential. Companies invested in data cleansing and validation processes, recognizing that accurate, high-quality data was critical to making reliable predictions and insights.

The rise of big data provided the essential fuel for machine learning's evolution. The combination of massive data volumes, diverse formats, and real-time processing enabled machine learning to become more accurate, adaptable, and impactful.

Integration of Big Data with Machine Learning

The synergy between big data and machine learning has transformed analytics and decision-making across industries. With advancements in data collection methods, machine learning models adapted to process and analyze unstructured data such as images, videos, and text. This shift empowered organizations to derive insights from previously untapped data sources, driving greater predictive accuracy and fostering innovation. Additionally, cloud computing played a vital role by providing scalable storage and enabling faster processing of massive datasets.

Technical Foundations: Algorithms and Models

In machine learning, algorithms are the core methods that define how data is processed, analyzed, and interpreted to make predictions or identify patterns. When algorithms are applied to specific data, they produce a 'model'—a structured representation of the insights extracted from that data. This model encapsulates patterns, trends, and relationships identified by the algorithm during its training process.

Essentially, a model is a mathematical construct that captures the underlying patterns in the data, enabling it to make predictions or decisions based on new, unseen data. For example, a model trained to recognize spam emails learns patterns from labeled emails, such as common keywords or sender behaviors. Once trained, the model can evaluate new emails and classify them accurately, applying the learned patterns without needing explicit rules for every scenario.

- **Decision Trees:** These were used for classification and regression tasks, breaking down complex decision-making processes into simpler, tree-like structures.
- **Support Vector Machines (SVMs):** SVMs became popular for classification tasks, especially in applications like image recognition.
- **Neural Networks:** Though still relatively simple, neural networks began to gain traction, with algorithms like backpropagation making training more effective.
- **K-Means Clustering:** Widely used for unsupervised learning, K-means clustering grouped data points based on similarity, helping with tasks like customer segmentation.

These foundational algorithms and models laid the groundwork for machine learning's evolution, enabling systems to recognize patterns and make predictions in increasingly complex tasks.

Real-World Applications: Machine Learning Across Industries

During this period, machine learning found its way into a wide range of industries, transforming everything from marketing to healthcare. Companies and organizations recognized the potential of machine learning to create predictive models, optimize processes, and improve decision-making.

1. **Finance:** Banks and financial institutions used machine learning for credit scoring, fraud detection, and algorithmic trading. By analyzing historical data, algorithms could detect unusual patterns indicative of fraud or forecast trends in stock prices.
2. **Healthcare:** Early applications in healthcare involved predictive modeling for disease outbreaks, patient risk assessment, and medical image analysis. Machine learning showed promise in diagnosing diseases from medical scans, laying the groundwork for future innovations in AI-driven diagnostics.
3. **Retail and Marketing:** E-commerce giants like Amazon and Walmart leveraged machine learning for recommendation systems, using customer data to personalize shopping experiences. Machine learning also improved demand forecasting, helping retailers optimize inventory and pricing.
4. **Transportation:** Machine learning algorithms helped optimize logistics, reducing fuel costs and improving route efficiency. These early applications in logistics and scheduling would later evolve into technologies enabling autonomous vehicles.
5. Telecommunications: Telecom companies leveraged machine learning for network optimization and predictive maintenance, enabling them to identify potential network issues and address them proactively, reducing downtime.

This widespread adoption laid a foundation for AI's further expansion, proving its ability to solve complex problems.

Technology Stack for Building ML Algorithms and Models

To develop and deploy machine learning (ML) solutions, a variety of programming languages and tools were used to define algorithms, build models, and bring them to life in practical applications

- **Python:** Started gaining popularity for machine learning in the 2000s, particularly with libraries like NumPy and SciPy (early versions). Toward the decade's end, Pandas began to support data manipulation, but Python's full ecosystem for machine learning matured in the early 2010s.
- **R:** Known for its statistical capabilities, R was extensively used in academia and research. Foundational packages like MASS enabled statistical analysis, and caret (introduced in 2006) became valuable for model training toward the end of the decade.
- **Java:** Java was widely used in enterprise environments, and Weka (a Java-based library) provided tools for implementing and testing machine learning algorithms, making Java suitable for academic and industrial research.
- **MATLAB:** Was a preferred tool in academia and engineering, with its Statistics and Machine Learning Toolbox offering a suite for algorithm development, data analysis, and model prototyping, particularly in scientific computing environments.
- **C++:** In the 2000s, C++ was essential for performance-intensive applications requiring high computational efficiency. Libraries like Shark (developed in 2004) and Dlib (released in 2003) supported the development of complex algorithms and models, particularly in scenarios where speed and resource optimization were crucial.

Supporting Infrastructure for Machine Learning

Machine learning models required foundational infrastructure for deployment, scalability, and efficient management. Key elements in this period focused on computational power, data storage, and early resource management.

- **High-Performance Computing (HPC):** Before the rise of fully managed cloud services, organizations relied on high-performance computing clusters for model training and deployment. Although cloud computing started in the 2000s, comprehensive ML services only emerged late
- **GPUs:** GPUs, especially from NVIDIA, gained traction for machine learning in the late 2000s. Originally built for graphics, they provided essential parallel processing to accelerate model training on large datasets.
- **Data Storage and Management:** Efficient data handling was critical. Hadoop (introduced in 2006) provided distributed storage and processing through HDFS, enabling organizations to manage large datasets effectively.
- **Virtualization:** Before containerization tools like Docker existed, virtualization allowed for isolated environments to deploy machine learning applications across different hardware configurations.
- **Data Warehousing and ETL** (Extract, Transform, Load) Processes: As organizations gathered more data, data warehousing solutions like Oracle, IBM DB2, and Microsoft SQL Server became essential for storing and managing structured datasets. ETL processes were widely used to collect, clean, and organize data, preparing it for analysis and machine learning tasks.

This infrastructure enabled the deployment and scaling of machine learning models with the tools available at the time, setting the stage for future advancements in AI infrastructure

Challenges and Limitations

Despite the progress, machine learning in the 2000s faced notable challenges

- **Computational Limitations:** Machine learning models, particularly neural networks, were often constrained by the computing power available. Training complex models was resource-intensive, limiting the speed and scalability of applications.
- **Data Privacy Concerns:** With the increasing amount of data collected, privacy concerns began to arise. Regulations like the European Data Protection Directive highlighted the need for data protection standards, foreshadowing future privacy laws.
- **Data Quality and Bias:** Models were only as good as the data they were trained on. Low-quality or biased data could lead to unreliable predictions, a challenge that would persist and grow as machine learning became more widespread.

The Shift Toward Data-Driven Decision-Making

As machine learning's impact grew, more organizations adopted data-driven strategies, relying on algorithms over intuition for decisions in areas from marketing to healthcare. This shift enabled businesses to make precise, objective, and timely choices, boosting their competitive edge.

Advancing Toward Deep Learning

The 2000s set the stage for deep learning, a powerful subset of machine learning that enabled AI systems to process vast data and tackle complex problems. This breakthrough would drive advances across fields like image recognition and language processing, redefining AI's potential.

CHAPTER ELEVEN

2010s: The Rise Of Deep Learning

In the early 2010s, while machine learning was effective for structured data, the growing need for AI systems to tackle complex tasks like image and speech recognition highlighted its limitations with unstructured data, leading researchers and tech giants to turn to new approach: deep learning

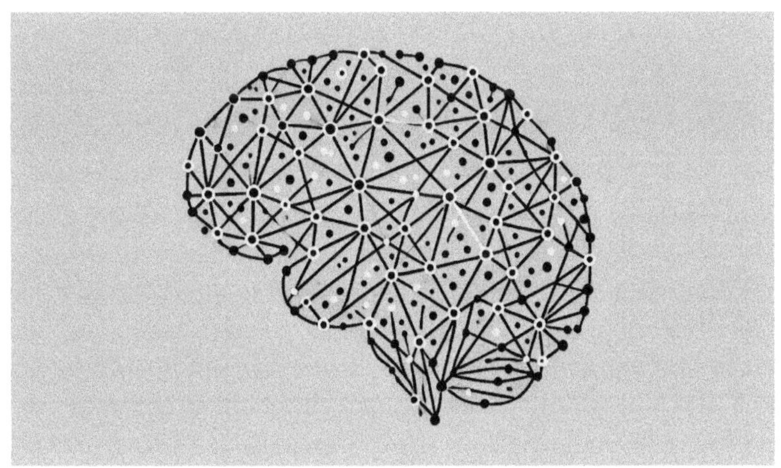

AI Representation of Human Brain and Neural Networks

Deep Learning Inspired by the Human Brain

The 2010s marked a transformative era in artificial intelligence, driven by the rise of deep learning—a powerful subset of machine learning inspired by the structure and functioning of the human brain. Deep learning relies on artificial neural networks, computational models designed to mimic how neurons in the brain process and transmit information. Just as human neurons activate and connect in complex ways to recognize patterns, deep learning models use layers of artificial "neurons" to analyze data, identify patterns, and make decisions.

Each layer in a deep neural network is designed to capture specific features from the input data, similar to how different regions of the human brain handle different aspects of visual or auditory processing. For example, in image recognition, initial layers might detect simple shapes and edges, while deeper layers capture more complex features, such as textures and shapes. This layered approach, often referred to as a "hierarchical" structure, enables deep learning models to process raw data in multiple steps, each one refining the model's understanding, much like the brain's processing hierarchy.

The rise of deep learning was made possible by improvements in computational power, especially with Graphics Processing Units (GPUs), which sped up the training of neural networks on large datasets. As these networks grew deeper—adding dozens or even hundreds of layers—they could handle complex tasks, such as identifying objects in images and translating languages. With access to massive datasets, deep learning models could learn and improve, achieving breakthroughs in areas once thought to need human intelligence, bringing machines closer to human-like understanding than ever before.

Key Differences Between Deep Learning and Machine Learning

Data Requirements: One of the most significant differences between machine learning and deep learning is the amount of data required. Traditional machine learning can work with relatively small datasets, but deep learning typically needs large amounts of data to function effectively, as it allows deep learning models to "learn" complex patterns and make more accurate predictions

Feature Engineering: In machine learning, feature selection and engineering are often done manually, requiring domain expertise to identify the most relevant features from the data. In deep learning, the algorithm automatically learns the features, making it less dependent on human input. This is especially beneficial for tasks like image recognition and natural language processing, where manually defining features can be complex and time-consuming.

Complexity and Interpretability: Deep learning models, particularly those with many layers, can be seen as "black boxes" because their decision-making process is difficult to interpret. This lack of transparency can be a disadvantage in areas where interpretability is important, such as healthcare and finance. In contrast, machine learning models tend to be more interpretable, as they are generally simpler and the relationships between input features and output predictions are more straightforward.

Accuracy and Versatility: Deep learning tends to outperform in tasks involving unstructured data or complex patterns. Deep learning has achieved significant breakthroughs in fields such as computer vision, natural language processing, and speech recognition, where traditional machine learning struggles. However, deep learning is not always the best choice for simpler tasks or smaller datasets

Computational Power: Deep learning models are computationally intensive and often require specialized hardware, such as GPUs (Graphics Processing Units) or TPUs (Tensor Processing Units), to handle the massive amounts of data and perform the necessary calculations. Machine learning, on the other hand, can often run on standard hardware, making it more accessible for smaller applications and less resource-demanding tasks.

Machine Learning Applications: Due to its structured approach and lower computational requirements, machine learning is commonly used in applications where well-defined data and straightforward patterns are present. Examples include customer segmentation, credit scoring, and predictive maintenance. In these scenarios, machine learning's speed and efficiency make it a practical choice.

Deep Learning Applications: Deep learning is ideal for complex tasks that involve unstructured data and require high accuracy. It is widely used in image recognition, speech recognition, natural language processing, and autonomous driving. For instance, deep learning models are at the core of virtual assistants like Siri and Alexa, as well as facial recognition technologies and real-time language translation.

Both machine learning and deep learning play essential roles in AI, each suited to different types of tasks and data. Machine learning offers a versatile and efficient approach for tasks with structured data and simpler patterns, while deep learning provides unmatched power for handling unstructured data and solving complex problems. Together, they represent a spectrum of AI capabilities that continue to drive innovation and transformation across industries.

Real-World Applications: Deep Learning Across Industries

Deep learning spread through various industries, revolutionizing how tasks were performed

- **Healthcare:** Deep learning algorithms enhanced medical imaging, detecting diseases like cancer with improved accuracy, facilitating early diagnosis and personalized treatment.
- **Automotive:** Autonomous driving relied on deep learning models to interpret sensor data, recognize objects, and make driving decisions, moving closer to fully self-driving vehicles.
- **Retail and E-commerce:** Companies like Amazon used deep learning for recommendation systems, personalizing customer experiences based on purchase history and browsing behavior.
- **Finance:** Fraud detection and algorithmic trading benefited from deep learning, enabling real-time analysis and rapid response to anomalies in financial data.
- **Entertainment and Media:** Deep learning-powered voice recognition systems, like Apple's Siri, enhanced user experiences, making technology more intuitive and accessible.

Deep learning's impact in the 2010s redefined industries, from healthcare diagnostics to autonomous driving and real-time financial analysis. Its ability to handle unstructured data also revolutionized language processing, enabling machines to interpret and respond to human speech.This paved the way for breakthroughs in Natural Language Processing (NLP), allowing AI to transform human-machine interactions into intuitive, conversational experiences, making technology more responsive and aligned with human communication.

CHAPTER TWELVE

2010s: The Rise Of Natural Language Processing (NLP)

Natural Language Processing (NLP) is a branch of artificial intelligence focused on enabling computers to understand, interpret, and generate human language. This technology helps machines make sense of text and speech, powering applications like language translation, voice assistants, and text analysis.

In the early 2010s, driven by deep learning advancements, NLP began processing language in a more natural and refined manner. Rather than relying on simple rules or patterns, new methods used large datasets and advanced neural networks to teach machines how to recognize context, tone, and meaning. This shift brought NLP closer to human-like comprehension, setting the stage for sophisticated AI-powered interactions like Siri, Alexa, and complex language models. Bridging the gap between human communication and machine understanding.

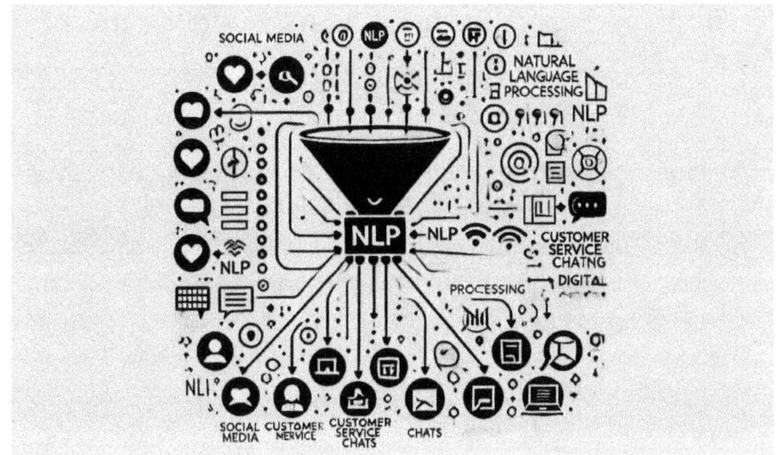

AI representation of data flow into (NLP)

Meeting the Demand for Human-Machine Communication

The 2010s brought an explosion of unstructured text data, driven by the rise of social media, messaging apps, and digital content. Every day, people produced vast amounts of text, from casual conversations to professional communications. This data created an urgent need for technologies that could interpret, analyze, and derive meaning from human language

As machines became more embedded in daily life, the demand for intuitive, human-like communication with technology increased. NLP emerged as the solution, bridging the gap between human expression and machine understanding

By advancing NLP capabilities, machines were better equipped to understand human language, making interactions feel more seamless, bridging gap between data and human expression.

Technology Stack for Building NLP Algorithms and Models

- **Python:** By the early 2010s, Python was becoming popular for NLP due to its readability and rich ecosystem. NLTK was a primary library, widely used in academia for tokenization, parsing, and classification tasks. scikit-learn supported machine learning tasks like text classification, and Gensim offered tools for topic modeling. These libraries formed the core NLP toolkit in Python before spaCy's release in 2015.
- **Java:** Java was widely used for NLP in enterprise settings for its scalability and performance. The Stanford NLP suite provided tools for tasks like part-of-speech tagging and named entity recognition, while Apache OpenNLP supported foundational NLP tasks in production. Both libraries were favored in large-scale applications, making Java a strong choice for backend NLP processing in the early 2010s.
- **While less prominent for mainstream NLP:** R was used in academia for text mining with packages like tm and SnowballC. Perl was favored for text manipulation in bioinformatics due to its regular expression capabilities. C++ supported performance-intensive tasks like machine translation with Moses, while SQL databases managed large text corpora and annotations. Early AWS offerings enabled larger-scale data storage and compute, though specialized NLP cloud tools were limited

As NLP evolved through the 2010s, the combination of open-source tools, scalable cloud infrastructure, and a growing ecosystem of machine learning libraries transformed the field. This period laid the groundwork for later advancements in deep learning and large-scale language models. Together, these technologies created a foundation for modern NLP applications in both research and industry

Real-World NLP Applications in the Early 2010s

In the early 2010s, real-world implementations of NLP were beginning to impact various industries.

AI representation of sentiment analysis - NLP

Companies used NLP to analyze public sentiment on social media platforms. Tools like Python's NLTK and early machine learning models helped businesses understand customer opinions, brand perception, and emerging trends, allowing them to adjust marketing strategies accordingly.

Customer Support Chatbots

Chatbots in the early 2010s were generally rule-based with limited NLP abilities, mainly using keyword matching and decision trees for basic customer inquiries.

AI representation of chatbots

Early rule-based chatbots provided basic customer service by handling simple, scripted interactions. These chatbots answered frequently asked questions or directed users to resources, offering an efficient, cost-effective support solution

Email Filtering and Spam Detection

NLP-based spam filtering was common, with models like Naive Bayes helping to classify emails as spam or non-spam.

AI representation of email filtering system

NLP helped classify emails as spam or non-spam using techniques like Naive Bayes and decision trees. Prominent email providers used these methods to filter out unwanted messages, improving inbox management.

The Transformative Role of NLP in the 2010s

Throughout the 2010s, Natural Language Processing (NLP) evolved from a niche technology to a foundational element of artificial intelligence, powering countless applications that reshape human-computer interaction. As seen in tools like sentiment analysis, chatbots, and spam detection, NLP enabled machines to process and interpret human language, opening new doors for communication between people and technology.

The decade's advancements in NLP set the stage for more intuitive AI systems, fostering a closer alignment between human expression and machine understanding. By the end of the decade, NLP's influence spanned industries, transforming fields as diverse as customer service, marketing, and content moderation, making AI a seamless part of daily digital interactions.

As we move into the next chapter, we'll explore how tech giants like Google, Microsoft, Amazon, and IBM spearheaded AI advancements from 2010 to 2022. These companies not only revolutionized AI through machine learning, natural language processing, and cloud-based services but also integrated these technologies into diverse industries, transforming modern life. Their contributions reveal the rapid pace of AI innovation and its profound impact on society during this transformative period.

CHAPTER THIRTEEN

2010-2022: Tech Giants Driving AI Evolution

This period marked a pivotal era for AI, driven by tech giants. These companies advanced machine learning, natural language processing, and cloud-based AI services, making AI more accessible across industries.

AI representation of MNC Software Company

Google

Google emerged as a leader in artificial intelligence, leveraging AI to transform products, services, and industries. Here's an overview of a few of Google's AI advancements during this period.

- **2011: Google Brain Project** - Initiated to advance deep learning and neural network research.Demonstrated capabilities in image recognition and other complex AI tasks.
- **2012: Cat Recognition Experiment** - Google Brain trained neural networks to recognize cats in YouTube videos without labeled data, showcasing the potential of unsupervised learning.
- **2015: TensorFlow** - Google released TensorFlow, an open-source deep learning framework, which became one of the most widely used AI tools in research and development.
- **2016: AlphaGo** - Google DeepMind's AlphaGo defeated a world champion Go player, marking a historic achievement in AI for strategic games.
- **2017: Transformer Architecture** - Google introduced the Transformer model in the paper "Attention Is All You Need," revolutionizing natural language processing (NLP) and becoming the foundation for models like BERT and GPT.
- **2018: BERT (Bidirectional Encoder Representations from Transformers)** - Developed to improve natural language understanding. Enabled Google Search to better understand context in queries, enhancing the relevance of search results.
- **2019: DeepMind's AlphaFold** - Solved a 50-year-old challenge in biology by predicting protein structures, showcasing AI's potential in scientific breakthroughs.
- **2020: LaMDA and Language Understanding**- Google advanced conversational AI with LaMDA (Language Model for Dialogue Applications), focusing on meaningful, context-aware dialogue.

Integration into Google Products:

- **Google Search:** Enhanced by BERT and RankBrain for understanding natural language queries.
- **Google Translate:** Improved through neural machine translation for more accurate translations.
- **Google Photos:** Used AI for automatic categorization, face recognition, and photo enhancements.
- **Google Assistant:** Expanded conversational capabilities, allowing natural interactions with users.
- **Self-Driving Cars:** Through Waymo, Google led advancements in autonomous vehicle technology.
- **Google Classroom:** Integrated AI to personalize learning and assist educators.
- **Google Lens:** Identified objects, text, and landmarks through images.
- **YouTube:** AI-Powered Recommendations, enhanced video suggestions.
- **Google Maps:** Traffic Predictions and Route Suggestion, real-time guidance.
- **Google Workspace :** Smart Reply, Provided quick, context-aware responses for emails. Smart Compose, Suggested full phrases and sentences while writing emails.
- **AI for Disaster Prediction:** Provided early flood warnings in vulnerable regions.
- **Project Euphonia:** Speech Recognition for Disabilities, improved accessibility for individuals with speech impairments.

Google's extensive use of artificial intelligence across its products and groundbreaking advancements in AI have not only redefined technology but also paved the way for future innovations that seamlessly integrate into our daily lives and various industries.

Microsoft

Microsoft made significant advancements in artificial intelligence (AI), establishing itself as a major player in the field. Its contributions spanned research, product integration, and partnerships, focusing on democratizing AI for businesses and consumers. Below are a few examples.

- **2013: Project Oxford** - Launched to develop AI services for vision, speech, and language understanding. Led to the development of tools like facial recognition APIs and speech-to-text services
- **2016: Microsoft Cognitive Services** - A suite of APIs enabling developers to add AI capabilities like facial recognition, sentiment analysis, and translation into applications. Democratized access to AI tools for businesses and developers.
- **2017: Introduction of Transformer Models** - Worked on transformer architectures, contributing to advancements in natural language processing. Released models for tasks like text summarization and sentiment analysis.
- **2018: Microsoft Translator** - Integrated AI-driven neural machine translation for more accurate and context-aware translations. Supported cross-language communication in products like Office and Teams.
- **2019: Turing Natural Language Generation (T-NLG)** - Developed one of the largest language models of its time, designed to improve natural language understanding across Microsoft products. Enhanced applications like Microsoft Word, Outlook, and Bing.
- **2020: Azure AI and Custom Vision** - Expanded Azure AI services, enabling developers to create custom computer vision models and integrate them into applications. Focused on enabling industries to solve domain-specific problems with AI.

Integration into Microsoft Products:

- **Cortana:** Enhanced with AI to serve as a virtual assistant across devices, integrating with Windows and Office 365.
- **Microsoft Office 365:** Incorporated AI for features like predictive typing, grammar correction, and personalized suggestions in tools like Word, Excel, and Outlook.
- **Microsoft Outlook:** Used AI to prioritize important emails. Provided AI-powered scheduling suggestions and email summaries.
- **Microsoft Teams:** AI-driven features included noise suppression, real-time transcription, and language translation.
- **Bing Search:** Improved with AI models for better natural language understanding and query interpretation.
- **Microsoft Edge Browser:** Used AI to organize and suggest content based on user behavior.
- **Windows Hello:** Introduced facial recognition and biometric authentication using AI.
- **Power BI:** AI-Powered Analytics, included natural language queries, automatic data pattern detection, and forecasting to simplify business intelligence and data visualization.
- Skype: AI-Powered Real-Time Translation, supported live language translation for calls and messages.
- **LinkedIn (Owned by Microsoft):** Leveraged AI to suggest professional connections, match job postings with suitable candidates, analyze and recommend courses based on user profiles and career goals.

Microsoft's pioneering contributions to AI have democratized its power, making transformative artificial intelligence technologies accessible to businesses and individuals, while shaping the future of AI-driven solutions.

IBM

IBM remained a leader in artificial intelligence (AI), IBM's advancements in AI centered around its Watson platform and its commitment to developing ethical, explainable AI for industries such as healthcare, finance, and retail. Below are a few examples.

- **2011: IBM Watson** - IBM Watson gained global attention by defeating human champions on the quiz show Jeopardy. Demonstrated Watson's ability to process and analyze natural language at scale, marking a significant milestone in AI's public visibility.
- **2014: Watson Health** - Focused on helping doctors and researchers analyze medical data for better diagnostics, drug discovery, and personalized treatment.
- **2016: IBM Watson IoT (Internet of Things)** - Enabled businesses to integrate IoT data with AI for predictive maintenance, supply chain optimization, and environmental monitoring. Helped industries analyze vast IoT datasets using Watson AI tools.
- **2017: Project Debater** - Introduced an AI capable of constructing arguments and engaging in debates with humans. Demonstrated the potential of AI to understand nuanced language and present coherent, persuasive arguments.
- **2018: OpenScale** - Developed as a platform for managing and monitoring AI deployments.
- **2018: AI for Cybersecurity (IBM QRadar Advisor)** - Launched a tool that used Watson to detect and analyze cybersecurity threats, Focused on automating threat detection and response.
- **2019: IBM Cloud Pak for Data** - A hybrid cloud platform that used AI to simplify data preparation, analysis, and deployment. Allowed organizations to integrate AI into workflows across multiple cloud environments.

IBM's AI Integration Across Industries:

- **Healthcare:** Watson for Oncology helped doctors analyze patient data and provide evidence-based treatment recommendations. Watson Health collaborated with major pharmaceutical companies to accelerate drug discovery using AI.
- **Finance:** AI tools powered fraud detection, credit risk analysis, and customer service for banks. Watson Assistant was used for conversational AI in customer support.
- **Retail:** AI-driven solutions optimized supply chain management, demand forecasting, and personalized shopping experiences. Watson Commerce enabled retailers to deliver tailored marketing campaigns based on customer insights.
- **Legal:** AI tools like ROSS Intelligence assisted lawyers by analyzing case law and providing relevant insights.
- **Education:** Watson Education to personalize learning experiences by analyzing student performance and providing tailored resources for improvement. It also enabled educators to identify learning gaps and predict student outcomes using AI-driven insights.
- **Agriculture:** Watson Decision Platform for Agriculture, which used AI to provide data-driven insights to farmers. By analyzing weather patterns, soil conditions, and crop data, the platform helped optimize planting schedules, improve yield predictions, and enhance supply chain management.

IBM's work during this decade emphasized leveraging AI for real-world problem-solving while promoting ethical and explainable AI. By focusing on enterprise applications and addressing AI challenges like bias and transparency, IBM helped shape AI's role in industries worldwide.

Amazon

Between 2010 and 2020, Amazon significantly advanced artificial intelligence (AI) by integrating it into its core business operations and developing innovative technologies. From e-commerce optimization to cloud-based AI services and voice assistants, Amazon played a key role in making AI accessible to businesses and consumers. Below are a few examples.

- **2014: Launch of Alexa and Echo Devices** - Amazon's AI-powered virtual assistant, along with Echo smart speakers. Revolutionized voice-based interactions and smart home integration, setting a new standard for conversational AI.
- **2015: AWS Machine Learning Services** - Expanded Amazon Web Services (AWS) to offer pre-trained AI models and custom machine learning tools. Enabled businesses to leverage AI for predictive analytics, recommendation engines, and more without needing in-house expertise.
- **2017: Amazon SageMaker** - Launched SageMaker as a fully managed service for building, training, and deploying machine learning models. Simplified AI adoption for developers by providing scalable infrastructure and integrated tools.
- **2018: Amazon Rekognition** - Introduced Rekognition, an AI-powered facial recognition and image analysis service. Used by industries for security, surveillance, and identifying objects or scenes in images and videos.
- **2018: Amazon Comprehend** - Released Comprehend, a natural language processing (NLP) service to analyze text for sentiment, key phrases, and topics. Empowered businesses to understand customer feedback and automate document processing.
- **2019: Personalize and Forecast** - A recommendation engine enabling businesses to deliver tailored content to users, powered by the same technology as Amazon's retail platform. Leveraged AI to predict demand, inventory needs, and financial outcomes for businesses.

Integration into Amazon Products and Diverse Industries:

- **E-Commerce:** AI optimized product recommendations, personalized shopping experiences, and dynamic pricing. Used demand forecasting and supply chain optimization to improve efficiency. AI-powered robots streamlined warehouse operations, boosting delivery speed and accuracy.
- **Smart Home Ecosystem:** Alexa powered smart home devices, enabling users to control lights, thermostats, and security systems through voice commands.
- **Media and Entertainment:** AI-driven algorithms on Amazon Prime Video personalized content recommendations. AWS provided backend AI services for video streaming, enhancing content delivery and user experiences.
- **Retail and Logistics:** Advanced robotics and machine learning were deployed in warehouses to automate inventory management. AI improved last-mile delivery by optimizing routes and vehicle usage.
- **Healthcare:** Launched AWS HealthLake in 2020 to store, transform, and analyze health data using AI. Explored AI-driven pharmacy solutions with Amazon Pharmacy.
- **AWS Marketplace for AI:** Provided a platform for businesses to access and deploy AI tools and algorithms easily.

Amazon's AI advancements during this decade transformed e-commerce, smart home technology, and cloud computing. By embedding AI in its services and products, Amazon not only reshaped consumer experiences but also made cutting-edge AI tools accessible to businesses worldwide, driving innovation across industries.

Facebook (Now Meta)

Between 2010 and 2022, Facebook (now Meta) advanced AI through innovations in natural language processing (e.g., translation tools), computer vision (e.g., automatic image tagging), and recommendation algorithms (e.g., personalized News Feed). It played a pivotal role in open-source AI with the launch of PyTorch in 2016, fostering global AI research, Below are a few examples.

- **2013: DeepFace** - Introduced DeepFace, a deep learning system for facial recognition with 97% accuracy, on par with human recognition. Applied in photo tagging and content moderation.
- **2018: M Translations** - Developed multilingual NLP models for real-time translations across Facebook, Instagram, and Messenger.
- **2020: Deep Learning Recommendation Model (DLRM)** - Built one of the most advanced recommendation models, powering personalized content and advertisements across Meta's platforms.
- **2021: SEER (Self-supervised Learning)** - Introduced a self-supervised computer vision model capable of recognizing objects in images without the need for labeled data, pushing the boundaries of unsupervised learning.

Applications:

- Personalized content in News Feeds through recommendation algorithms.
- AI-driven ad targeting for businesses, enhancing revenue and engagement.
- Real-time content moderation to detect hate speech, misinformation, and harmful content.

Apple

Apple has consistently leveraged artificial intelligence to revolutionize user experiences across its ecosystem of devices. From pioneering voice interactions with Siri to integrating on-device machine learning for enhanced privacy and performance, Apple has seamlessly blended AI into everyday applications. Below are a few examples.

- **2011: Siri** - Introduced Siri, one of the first widely used AI voice assistants, enabling natural language interactions.
- **2013: Touch ID** - Introduced AI-powered fingerprint recognition for enhanced device security and seamless user authentication.
- **2017: Face ID** - Launched facial recognition powered by advanced AI and neural networks, **enabling secure authentication and payment processing.**

Applications:

- AI-powered user experiences in devices like iPhone, iPad, and Apple Watch.
- Features like real-time translation, health tracking, and fitness recommendations.
- Enhanced computational photography in iPhone cameras, using AI to improve image quality and depth.

Chapter Conclusion : The 2010–2022 era solidified the role of AI as a transformative force, thanks to the pioneering efforts of tech giants like Google, Microsoft, Amazon, IBM, and more. Their innovations not only reshaped industries but also laid the groundwork for the next wave of AI advancements.

2010-2022: AI Startups Revolution

Overview of the rise of AI startups during 2010-2022: Between 2010 and 2022, AI startups emerged as catalysts for groundbreaking innovation, driving advancements that redefined what AI could achieve.

AI representation of Startup Workspace

OpenAI

Founded in 2015, OpenAI is a leading AI research organization that has driven significant advancements in artificial intelligence. With a mission to ensure AI benefits all of humanity, OpenAI pioneered groundbreaking technologies, including Large Language Models (LLMs) like GPT-3, and focused on creating safe and ethical AI systems.

- **Founded Year:** 2015
- **Purpose:** To advance digital intelligence in a way that is safe and beneficial for humanity, ensuring AI systems align with human values.
- **Key Products:** GPT-2 and GPT-3, Generative pre-trained models that redefined conversational AI and content generation. DALL·E: An AI system for generating images from textual descriptions, pushing the boundaries of creative AI. Codex: An AI-powered coding assistant, enabling natural language programming capabilities.
- **Problems Solved:** OpenAI addressed the challenge of creating AI systems that could understand and generate human-like text, enabling applications in content creation, virtual assistants, and automation. Their focus on ethical AI also tackled concerns about AI misuse and alignment with societal values.
- **Impact:** Revolutionized content creation, art generation, and storytelling through tools like DALL·E and GPT-3. Codex has significantly enhanced productivity for developers by automating coding tasks, reducing barriers to entry in programming.

Through their innovative models, ethical AI focus, OpenAI set new standards in AI research and applications. Their contributions continue to influence industries and shape the future of AI.

DeepMind

Founded in 2010, DeepMind is a British AI research company recognized for its groundbreaking work in artificial intelligence. Driven by a mission to solve intelligence and apply it to advance science and humanity, DeepMind has consistently pushed the boundaries of AI innovation in areas such as reinforcement learning and computational biology.

- **Founded Year:** 2010
- **Purpose:** To develop general-purpose AI systems capable of solving real-world challenges while advancing scientific discovery for the betterment of humanity.
- **Key Products**: AlphaGo, the first AI to defeat a world champion in the complex board game Go, demonstrating advanced capabilities in reinforcement learning. AlphaFold: Revolutionized biology by accurately predicting protein structures, accelerating breakthroughs in medicine and drug discovery.AlphaZero: A self-learning system mastering chess, shogi, and Go without human data, showcasing general AI adaptability.
- **Problems Solved:** DeepMind addressed the challenge of creating AI systems capable of learning and problem-solving with minimal human input. Their technologies advanced reinforcement learning, self-learning AI, and scientific research, unlocking solutions in fields such as biology and gaming.
- **Impact:** DeepMind's AlphaGo marked a historic milestone in AI, while AlphaFold transformed biological research and medical discovery. AlphaZero showcased the potential of AI to adapt and excel across multiple domains.

Acquired by Google in 2014, DeepMind continues to lead AI research globally, driving innovation in science and technology while inspiring future advancements in artificial intelligence.

Scale AI

Founded in 2016, Scale AI has played a pivotal role in accelerating AI advancements by specializing in data annotation and labeling for machine learning models. With a mission to make AI systems more accurate and effective, Scale AI has become a trusted partner for leading organizations in the AI ecosystem.

- **Founded Year:** 2016
- **Purpose:** To provide high-quality labeled data to train and improve machine learning models, enabling faster and more precise AI development.
- **Key Products:** Nucleus: A platform for managing and visualizing datasets, streamlining the data pipeline for machine learning projects. Scale Rapid: A tool for quick data labeling at scale, tailored for industries requiring fast iterations in AI model training. Autonomous Vehicle Data Services: Specialized in annotating data for self-driving technology, helping companies refine their autonomous systems.
- **Problems Solved:** Scale AI addressed the challenge of preparing high-quality training data for machine learning, which is often labor-intensive and time-consuming. By combining human expertise with automation, the company enabled efficient and scalable data labeling, critical for AI advancements in industries like autonomous vehicles, robotics, and NLP.
- **Impact:** Scale AI became instrumental in driving breakthroughs in conversational AI, self-driving technology, and computer vision. Its innovative tools and services streamlined AI development processes, setting new benchmarks for data quality and efficiency.

Scale AI's contributions highlight the importance of quality data in AI innovation. Its services continue to power some of the most advanced AI applications.

Runway

Founded in 2018, Runway revolutionized the creative industry by offering AI tools tailored for content creators. By leveraging generative AI for video, images, and audio, Runway enabled artists, designers, and filmmakers to push creative boundaries and streamline workflows.

- **Founded Year:** 2018
- **Purpose:** To empower creators with innovative AI tools that enhance productivity and unlock new possibilities in media and design.
- **Key Products:** Runway Video Tools, generative AI solutions for video editing, enabling automated scene generation, background removal, and special effects. Image Generation Tools: AI-powered tools for creating high-quality, photorealistic images and illustrations. Audio Editing AI: Advanced features for sound design, including AI-assisted voice synthesis and noise reduction.
- **Problems Solved:** Runway addressed the creative industry's need for efficient tools to produce high-quality content quickly. By introducing generative AI capabilities, it reduced the time and effort required for complex editing tasks, making advanced creative techniques accessible to a broader audience.
- **Impact:** Runway's tools have been widely adopted in media, advertising, and entertainment, transforming how creators develop content. Its innovative solutions have empowered independent artists and large production teams alike.

Runway's commitment to bridging AI and creativity has cemented its role as a pioneer in the AI-driven creative industry. Its tools continue to inspire and support creators worldwide, driving innovation in digital content creation.

Replit AI

Founded in 2016, Replit AI revolutionized software development and education by integrating artificial intelligence into its collaborative coding platform. With a vision to make programming accessible to everyone, Replit AI empowered developers and learners through innovative AI-powered tools.

- **Founded Year:** 2016
- Purpose: To democratize software development by providing accessible, AI-driven coding tools for developers, educators, and learners.
- **Key Products:** Ghostwriter, An AI coding assistant that offers real-time code suggestions, bug fixes, and explanations, enhancing productivity and learning. Collaborative Coding Platform: A cloud-based environment where users can write, debug, and deploy code with AI support. AI-Driven Learning Features: Tools to simplify coding concepts for beginners and enable hands-on programming education.
- **Problems Solved:** Replit AI addressed challenges in software development by streamlining the coding process with AI-powered assistance. It reduced barriers for beginners, enhanced efficiency for experienced developers, and simplified collaboration for teams.
- **Impact:** Replit AI transformed how coding is taught and practiced, enabling millions of users worldwide to create and learn more efficiently. Ghostwriter has become a key tool for boosting productivity and fostering innovation among developers, educators, and students.

Through its AI-driven platform and tools like Ghostwriter, Replit AI has made coding more inclusive, accessible, and engaging, setting new standards in the intersection of AI and software development.

MidJourney

Founded in 2022, MidJourney revolutionized the field of creative AI with its generative image synthesis platform. Focused on empowering creators and artists, MidJourney enabled users to generate stunning, high-quality visuals from text prompts, pushing the boundaries of art and design.

- **Founded Year:** 2022
- Purpose: To democratize creativity by providing AI-powered tools for generating visually striking images from natural language descriptions.
- **Key Products:** Generative AI Platform, allows users to create unique, high-resolution artwork and designs with simple text inputs. Offers users control over artistic styles, colors, and compositions to tailor outputs to specific needs. Facilitates teamwork in creative projects by enabling shared prompts and iterative feedback.
- **Problems Solved:** MidJourney addressed the challenge of creating art quickly and at scale without requiring advanced design skills. It bridged the gap between artistic vision and execution, enabling creators to bring ideas to life efficiently.
- **Impact:** MidJourney transformed creative workflows, becoming a go-to tool for artists, marketers, and designers. Its ability to generate diverse visuals enhanced productivity in industries like advertising, gaming, and media, while inspiring new forms of digital art.

By combining the cutting-edge generative Artificial Intelligence with user-friendly design, MidJourney has redefined artistic expression through images, opening new avenues for creativity and innovation, setting new standards in the field of text-to-image generation.

Hugging Face

Founded in 2016, Hugging Face is a trailblazing AI startup recognized for its contributions to natural language processing (NLP) and open-source AI development. Initially known for creating a chatbot app, Hugging Face transitioned into a global leader in NLP tools and frameworks, democratizing AI for researchers, developers, and businesses.

- **Founded Year:** 2016
- **Purpose:** To build accessible and open-source tools that enable advancements in NLP and AI, fostering collaboration and innovation within the global AI community.
- **Key Products:** Transformers Library - An open-source platform for training and deploying state-of-the-art NLP models like BERT, GPT, and RoBERTa. Datasets Library: A repository for standardized datasets, enabling faster and more efficient AI model development. Hugging Face Hub: A collaborative platform for sharing and hosting pre-trained AI models, supporting both individuals and organizations in deploying AI solutions.
- **Problems Solved:** Hugging Face addressed the need for accessible NLP tools and frameworks, making it easier to train, fine-tune, and deploy advanced language models. Their open-source approach lowered barriers for researchers and developers, accelerating innovation across industries.
- **Impact:** Hugging Face revolutionized how AI models are developed and shared, empowering users to create applications in translation, summarization, sentiment analysis, and more. Their platforms became essential resources for researchers and developers, driving progress in academia and industry alike.

Through its focus on collaboration, openness, and innovation, Hugging Face has established itself as a cornerstone of the AI community, shaping the future of NLP and AI research.

Startup Aquisitions

Between 2010 and 2022, major technology companies actively acquired numerous AI startups to enhance their capabilities and maintain competitive advantages. Notable acquisitions include

- **Google:** Aquired DeepMind (2014) , Kaggle (2017), Alooma (2019)
- **Apple:** Aquired Turi (2016), Xnor.ai (2020), Inductiv (2020)
- **Microsoft:** Aquired Maluuba (2017), Bonsai (2018), Lobe (2018)
- **Facebook (now Meta):** Aquired Ozlo (2017), Bloomsbury AI (2018)
- **Amazon:** Aquired Orbeus (2016), Harvest.ai (2017)

These acquisitions reflect the strategic efforts of tech giants to integrate advanced AI technologies, driving innovation and maintaining leadership in the rapidly evolving AI landscape.

Chapter Conclusion

The chapter highlights the transformative journey of AI startups between 2010 and 2022, showcasing their groundbreaking contributions to AI advancements. These startups redefined industries by developing innovative technologies, from generative AI to tools for data annotation and content creation, significantly shaping the AI ecosystem. Through their agility and vision, they addressed challenges in diverse domains, pioneering solutions that resonated globally. The era underscored the pivotal role of startups in pushing AI's boundaries, leaving a lasting impact on both the tech landscape and broader societal advancements.

CHAPTER FIFTEEN

2010-2022: The Unnoticed AI

In the late 2000s, AI technologies like machine learning (ML), natural language processing (NLP), and early deep learning was mostly confined to businesses and research labs, where it shaped industries through data analysis and automation.it hadn't yet reached the daily lives of most people. During the 2010s, however, AI began to touch the lives of regular people, subtly integrating into consumer technologies and personal devices.

In this era, AI moved from back-end systems to the forefront of user experiences, powering voice assistants like Siri and Alexa, personalizing recommendations on streaming platforms like Netflix and Spotify, and optimizing our social media feeds. These applications made AI a silent but constant presence in our routines, guiding decisions and enhancing convenience—often without us realizing the level of intelligence working behind the scenes. As AI seamlessly integrated into our devices and applications, it became a quiet force shaping how we communicated, consumed content, and interacted with the digital world, adapting to our preferences and habits in ways that felt almost intuitive. The presence of AI in everyday life was subtle yet impactful, marking a shift where technology began to anticipate our needs, making it feel almost invisible while transforming our digital interactions.

Unnoticed AI: Quietly Present in Our Daily Live

AI quietly became an integral part of many sectors. In healthcare, AI supported diagnostics, from interpreting medical images to predicting disease patterns, while also optimizing hospital operations and personalizing treatment plans. In finance, AI-powered algorithms detected fraud, managed risks, and even automated trading, allowing for faster and more accurate decision-making.

Beyond these areas, AI's impact was felt in industries like agriculture, where it monitored crop health and optimized harvests, and in transportation, where it enabled autonomous driving technologies and improved traffic management. In retail and e-commerce, AI enhanced user experiences by personalizing product recommendations, streamlining inventory management. Even in education, AI-powered personalized learning, adjusting content to individual student needs, and in environmental science, AI models helped monitor wildlife and track climate changes. These applications showed AI working behind the scenes, enhancing efficiency and providing insights across diverse domains.

AI representation of voice assistant

Voice Assistants

- **Voice Assistants:** Siri, Google Assistant – interpreting voice commands, understanding natural language, they personalize user interactions by learning preferences and adapting responses over time.
- **Functionality:** Voice assistants like Siri and Google Assistant can interpret voice commands to perform tasks such as setting reminders, sending messages, controlling smart devices, providing information, and answering questions.
- **Technology:** Voice Assistants utilize AI technologies like Speech Recognition, Natural Language Processing (NLP), Deep Learning, and Machine Learning.

Voice assistants have made life easier by handling everyday tasks effortlessly, They save time and streamline routines, allowing people to focus on what matters most.

AI representation of voice-activated ceiling fan

Smart Homes : AI Voice Assistants

- **Smart Homes:** AI Voice Assistants like Alexa – controlling home devices through voice, understanding user preferences to create a seamless living environment.
- **Functionality:** Smart home systems powered by voice assistants like Alexa can control lights, thermostats, security systems, and even appliances, providing automation and convenience.
- **Technology:** These systems utilize AI technologies like Speech Recognition, NLP, Deep Learning, and IoT to interpret commands and manage smart devices.

AI has made daily life more comfortable by automating routines, saving energy, and enhancing security, creating a truly connected and efficient home experience.

AI representation of family watching a streaming platform

- **Streaming Platforms:** Netflix, Spotify personalizing recommendations, analyzing viewing habits, and adapting content suggestions based on user preferences and engagement.
- **Functionality:** Streaming Platforms use AI to analyze viewing and listening habits, understanding preferences based on the content users watch, listen to, or interact with. By tracking genres, viewing times, and user ratings, they can predict what each person is likely to enjoy and present tailored recommendations.
- **Technology:** Streaming platforms utilize AI technologies like Machine Learning, Collaborative Filtering, Deep Learning, and Natural Language Processing (NLP) for recommendation algorithms and data analysis.

Streaming platforms have transformed entertainment by providing curated content, saving users time in finding what to watch or listen to, and enriching their media experiences.

AI representation of Social Media and Content Curation

- **Social Media Platforms:** Facebook, Instagram – AI-powered personalization enhances engagement by analyzing user behavior and displaying content aligned with individual interests
- **Functionality:** AI curates posts, ads, and recommendations to match user preferences and interaction patterns, while filtering out inappropriate or harmful content. This reduces the need for manual oversight, improves user safety, and delivers a more tailored, engaging experience.
- **Technology:** Social media platforms utilize AI technologies like Machine Learning, Natural Language Processing (NLP), Computer Vision, Deep Learning, Sentiment Analysis, and Recommendation Algorithms to analyze data and personalize content feeds.

AI on social media enhances the user experience by creating a dynamic, relevant feed that aligns with each person's unique interests and social connections.

AI representation of doctor and patient reviewing lab report

- **Healthcare and Diagnostics:** Medical Imaging, Predictive Healthcare, and Drug Discovery.
- **Functionality:** In medical imaging, AI analyzes X-rays, MRIs, and CT scans, helping detect anomalies and aiding doctors in accurate diagnoses. Predictive healthcare uses AI to assess patient risks and suggest preventive measures, while in drug discovery, AI accelerates the process by analyzing complex biological data.
- **Technology:** Healthcare applications use AI technologies like Computer Vision, Machine Learning, and Deep Learning to analyze medical data and personalize treatment plans. Convolutional Neural Networks (CNNs), a deep learning model, are especially effective in medical imaging, detecting conditions from fractures to tumors by analyzing X-rays, MRIs, and CT scans

AI in healthcare enhances diagnostic accuracy, enables proactive treatment, and accelerates drug development.

AI representation of space technology

- **Space Technology:** AI helps in Autonomous Decision-Making and Data Analysis
- **Functionality:** It also supports hazard detection, such as identifying near-Earth objects (NEOs) and avoiding space debris, helping to protect both Earth and satellites. It enables autonomous decision-making for satellites and rovers, allowing them to navigate, prioritize data, and adjust operations without constant human input.
- **Technology:** Space applications use AI technologies like Computer Vision, Machine Learning, and Deep Learning, enabling autonomous navigation, predictive maintenance, and real-time data analysis for satellite and planetary missions.

AI in space has enhanced mission efficiency, accelerated discoveries, and enabled safer, more efficient operations. It helps monitor spacecraft health, optimize resources, and provide real-time insights, advancing space exploration and research

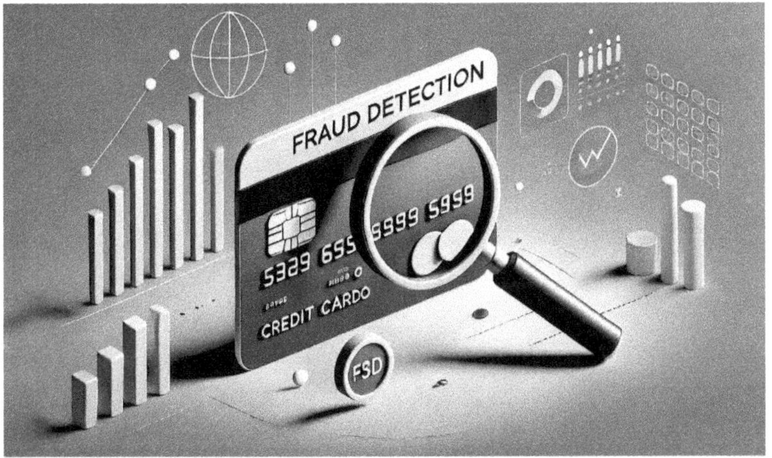

AI representation of fraud detection

- **Financial Services:** Algorithmic Trading, and Customer Support, Fraud Detection AI continuously monitors financial transactions, detecting unusual patterns and alerting institutions to prevent potential fraud in real-time.
- **Functionality:** AI in finance enables algorithmic trading by analyzing vast market data, executing trades precisely, and optimizing financial decisions. Additionally, chatbots support customer service by handling inquiries, managing accounts, and facilitating routine transactions.
- **Technology:** Financial services use AI technologies like Machine Learning, Natural Language Processing (NLP), and Deep Learning to detect fraud, manage trading algorithms, and enhance customer interactions, making transactions secure and efficient.

AI has improved financial security, streamlined customer service, and optimized investment strategies, creating safer and more accessible financial experiences.

AI representation of facial recognition in airports

- **Policing and Public Safety:** AI technologies enhance public safety by analyzing crime data, enabling proactive law enforcement through predictive policing strategies, which forecast potential crime hotspots.
- **Functionality:**Tools like facial recognition and behavior analysis systems assist in surveillance at airports, public spaces, and large events, improving security measures and identifying potential threats. AI also supports emergency response by prioritizing calls and dispatching resources swiftly for efficient incident handling.
- **Technology:** AI in policing uses Machine Learning, Computer Vision, and Natural Language Processing (NLP) to analyze patterns, recognize faces, and manage critical response systems effectively.

AI-driven public safety initiatives streamline crime prevention, surveillance, and emergency response, fostering safer communities and enhancing law enforcement capabilities.

Additional Examples of AI Applications

- **Education:** Adaptive learning platforms tailored lessons based on students performance and learning pace.
- **Manufacturing:** AI predicted machinery breakdowns, optimizing maintenance schedules to reduce downtime and costs and Predictive Maintenance,Supply Chain Optimization.
- **Agriculture**: AI analyzed soil health, crop conditions, and weather patterns to optimize farming practices and boost yield, AI-driven robots for crop harvesting.
- **Environmental Monitoring**: AI tracked pollution levels, climate changes, and deforestation, assisting in conservation efforts and policy decisions.
- **Real Estate:** AI analyzed market trends to predict property values, and virtual assistants helped potential buyers find properties that matched their preferences and budget.
- **Beauty and Cosmetics:** AI analyze skin types to recommend personalized skincare routines.
- **Fitness :** AI-driven virtual trainers provide real-time feedback on form and technique, simulating the experience of having a personal coach at home.

The journey through AI applications in diverse fields has highlighted how deeply AI has woven itself into the fabric of our lives. From enhancing daily conveniences through voice assistants and smart homes to driving significant advancements in healthcare, finance, and environmental monitoring, AI has become an integral yet often unseen force. As we continue to innovate, AI's role will only grow, further shaping our future and reinforcing its presence in ways we may not always notice, but certainly benefit from.

CHAPTER SIXTEEN

2022: The Rise Of ChatGPT and LLM's

Large Language Models (LLMs) emerged as groundbreaking AI systems, with OpenAI's GPT in 2018 leading the way. Unlike earlier NLP models, GPT leveraged transformer architecture and extensive datasets, Each successive version, including GPT-2 and GPT-3, further expanded LLM capabilities, paving the way for conversational AI like ChatGPT in 2022.

LLMs are designed to interpret and generate language that mimics human conversation, drawing from vast amounts of text to understand grammar, context, and subtle meanings. This allows them to perform a wide range of tasks, from answering questions to generating creative content, using deep neural networks that capture intricate language patterns.

Traditional AI models focused on specific, rule-based tasks with limited datasets. LLMs, however, are trained on broad, diverse sources, granting them flexibility to tackle varied topics and respond in contextually nuanced ways. This adaptability marked a major shift in AI's approach to understanding human language.

The Emergence of ChatGPT

- **Launch:** ChatGPT was officially launched by OpenAI on November 30, 2022.
- **Background:** OpenAI developed ChatGPT as part of its efforts to advance natural language processing and make AI more accessible to the public.
- **Technology:** ChatGPT uses a Large Language Model (LLM) architecture, specifically designed to process and generate text based on vast datasets. The model leverages transformer-based neural networks, which analyze patterns in language to predict and generate coherent, context-aware responses. This allows ChatGPT to simulate human-like conversation, adapting its answers based on the context and flow of interaction.
- **Initial public reaction:** ChatGPT gained rapid popularity, attracting over a million users within its first five days. The model's ability to engage in conversational dialogue and provide detailed responses captured public interest, sparking discussions across social media and tech communities.
- **Impact on Various Industries:** ChatGPT quickly found applications across diverse fields, from content creation and customer support to coding assistance and educational tutoring. This versatility showcased the potential of conversational AI to transform multiple industries.

GPT stands for Generative Pre-trained Transformer. It is a type of AI model developed by OpenAI that generates human-like text based on input prompts. **"Generative"** refers to its ability to produce text, **"Pre-trained"** means it's trained on vast datasets before being fine-tuned for specific tasks, and **"Transformer"** refers to the neural network architecture it uses, which excels at understanding and generating language by processing context within text.

How ChatGPT Works

ChatGPT is built on a transformer-based architecture, which is designed for processing sequences of text. The model has layers of "attention mechanisms" that allow it to weigh the importance of different words in a sentence, based on context. This process, known as self-attention, helps the model understand relationships between words, even if they are far apart in the text. When training, the model learns these patterns by analyzing vast datasets, adjusting millions (or even billions) of parameters within its layers to improve its accuracy. When a prompt is entered, ChatGPT uses these parameters to predict the next word, generating a response by iteratively selecting each word based on prior ones until a coherent sentence is formed. This structure allows ChatGPT to produce contextually relevant and conversational responses.

The training process for LLMs like ChatGPT involves feeding the model massive datasets composed of diverse text sources, such as books, websites, and articles, to expose it to a wide range of language patterns and topics. During training, the model adjusts its parameters—numerical weights that determine how strongly it responds to certain words or patterns—across billions of connections in its neural network. These parameters enable the model to make accurate predictions about language. The process is highly resource-intensive, often requiring powerful computational infrastructure to handle the scaling necessary for effective language comprehension. As the model trains, it progressively "learns" to generate more coherent and contextually accurate responses, making it capable of sophisticated conversational abilities.

ChatGPT's underlying transformer architecture and extensive training process empower it to generate coherent, contextually relevant responses, mimicking human-like conversation

Challenges and Limitations : Issues with LLMs

- **Bias and ethical concerns:** LLMs arise from the vast datasets used during training, which often contain biases present in real-world language. Since these models learn patterns from this data, they can inadvertently reproduce or amplify stereotypes and prejudiced views.
- **Misinformation:** LLMs, sometimes generate responses that sound believable but are factually incorrect, a phenomenon known as "hallucination." This can lead to the spread of misinformation, especially if users rely on the model for accurate answers.
- **Data Privacy:** LLMs rely heavily on large datasets for training, which raises concerns about data privacy and security. Ensuring privacy involves strict data handling practices and exploring techniques like differential privacy to protect user information in AI systems.
- **Resource Intensity:** Training and operating large language models demand significant computational power and resources, leading to high energy consumption. This resource intensity contributes to environmental concerns due to the carbon footprint of data centers. As AI technology advances, there is a growing focus on optimizing models to reduce their energy requirements and improve efficiency.
- **Difficulty with Niche Knowledge:** While LLMs perform well on general knowledge, they may struggle with niche or specialized domains due to limited data exposure in these areas. This can lead to less accurate or incomplete responses when addressing specialized topics.

These challenges highlight the limitations and concerns that come with using large language models.

The Dawn of Conversational AI

In 2022, ChatGPT and large language models (LLMs) brought a breakthrough in AI, transforming human-computer interaction with conversational and context-aware capabilities. By bridging the gap between complex machine processing and intuitive communication, these models made AI assistance more accessible and relevant across diverse areas like education, business, and everyday life. The rapid adoption of ChatGPT highlighted the demand for AI-driven tools that can engage with users in natural, human-like ways.

LLMs have redefined digital communication by providing responses that feel increasingly personalized and adaptable. Through vast datasets and context-based learning, models like ChatGPT offer smoother, more interactive experiences, making technology feel more intuitive. This shift has inspired excitement for future advancements in AI, where machines will not only assist but enhance the quality of human interactions, paving the way for intelligent, responsive systems.

As LLMs continue to evolve, they open a new chapter in the way we connect with technology, making it more conversational and accessible. These advancements have fueled curiosity about the future of AI-driven solutions, promising innovations that could further transform the digital landscape and redefine our daily interactions with AI.

Understanding - Ai Vs Generative Ai

Artificial Intelligence (AI) has become a transformative force across industries, automating processes, enhancing decision-making, and improving efficiency. Within AI, Generative AI (Gen AI) is an advanced subset that focuses on creating new content, such as images, text, and audio, rather than just analyzing data or performing tasks. While both share a common foundation, their purposes and applications highlight key differences.

AI encompasses a broad range of technologies designed to simulate human intelligence. It powers systems like recommendation engines, predictive analytics, and autonomous vehicles, which focus on problem-solving, pattern recognition, and task automation. Traditional AI models are trained to analyze data, identify patterns, and provide accurate outputs based on predefined rules or learning algorithms. These systems are vital for streamlining workflows and improving operational efficiency.

Generative AI, on the other hand, specializes in creativity. It uses deep learning models like Generative Adversarial Networks (GANs) and transformer architectures to generate original outputs, such as text-to-image creations, conversational responses, or even music compositions. Notable examples include ChatGPT for natural language generation and DALL·E for creating visuals from textual descriptions. Generative AI is revolutionizing industries like content creation, design, and entertainment by pushing creative boundaries.

In conclusion, while AI focuses on performing tasks and solving problems, Generative AI opens new avenues for creativity and innovation, marking a significant evolution in artificial intelligence.

Understanding Ai Risks

As Artificial Intelligence (AI) becomes a transformative force across industries, it brings with it significant challenges that require careful consideration. These risks, while varied, often center around ethical dilemmas, societal impact, and technological reliability.

- Bias and Fairness: AI systems, trained on historical data, can inherit and amplify existing biases. This has led to unequal outcomes in areas such as hiring, lending, and law enforcement, raising questions about fairness and accountability.
- Data Privacy: AI relies heavily on vast datasets, which often include sensitive personal information. Inadequate safeguards can result in breaches, misuse, or unauthorized access, jeopardizing individual privacy.
- Misinformation: Generative AI tools, like deepfakes, can produce convincing but false content, eroding trust in media and complicating efforts to discern tr
- Lack of Explainability: Many AI models, especially neural networks, operate as "black boxes," making it difficult to understand their decision-making processes and creating accountability challenges.

The Path Forward

Addressing these risks requires a collaborative approach, involving governments, industries, and civil society to ensure AI's development aligns with ethical, transparent, and human-centric principles

Ai Governance

As Artificial Intelligence (AI) becomes more central to industries and daily life, having clear rules and guidelines to govern its use is more important than ever. AI governance involves creating policies and regulations to ensure AI is used ethically, transparently, and responsibly. It focuses on addressing challenges like bias in algorithms, protecting privacy, ensuring accountability, and preventing misuse while balancing innovation with public good.

Effective governance combines ethical, technical, and legal efforts. It promotes transparency so people understand how AI makes decisions and ensures organizations are accountable for its outcomes. Collaboration among governments, businesses, researchers, and communities is key to creating standards that reflect shared values.

As AI evolves, some countries have already implemented laws to ensure it benefits society fairly and ethically. Here are examples of such implemented laws, while others remain in draft.

Currently Enforced AI Laws, Policy and Guidelines

- General Data Protection Regulation (GDPR) in European Union
- Ethics Guidelines for Trustworthy AI (2019) in European Union
- National AI Initiative Act (2021) and California Consumer Privacy Act (CCPA) in USA
- AI Ethics Guidelines (2021) in China
- Directive on Automated Decision-Making - Policy (2019) in Canada
- Digital Personal Data Protection Bill (2023) in India

Technology-focused Ai Businesses

Artificial Intelligence (AI) has opened diverse avenues for businesses, each leveraging unique technological capabilities.

- **Building Large Language Models (LLMs)** : Focused on developing foundational AI models like GPT, BERT, or PaLM, capable of natural language understanding and generation. Eg: OpenAI, Anthropic.
- **Leveraging LLMs and Building Tools** : Creating applications, APIs, and platforms that use LLMs for specific use cases like chatbots, summarization tools, or document generation. Eg: Jasper AI, Replit Ghostwriter.
- **Data Scraping and Annotation** : Collecting, cleaning, and labeling data required for training AI models or providing these as services. Eg: Scale AI, Appen.
- **AI Infrastructure and Cloud Services** : Providing platforms, hardware, or environments for training, deploying, and running AI models at scale. Eg: NVIDIA (GPUs), Google Cloud AI, AWS AI.
- **Autonomous Systems Development** : Building AI systems for autonomous vehicles, robotics, and drones using reinforcement learning and computer vision. Eg: Tesla, Boston Dynamics.
- **Custom AI Model Fine-Tuning** : Adapting pre-trained LLMs or vision models to industry-specific needs, such as healthcare or finance. Example: Hugging Face (Transformers library).
- **Generative AI Applications** : Using pre-trained models to build creative tools for generating text, images, audio, or video content. Eg: MidJourney, Runway.
- **AI Monitoring and Explainability Tools:** Developing solutions for tracking, explaining, and auditing AI model behavior to ensure accountability and reduce bias. Eg: Fiddler AI, Arize AI.
- **Conversational AI and Virtual Agents** : Leveraging AI to build virtual assistants, customer support bots, and conversational

platforms. Eg: Yellow.ai, Kore.ai.

- **AI-Powered Analytics and Decision-Making Platforms** : Building platforms that apply AI for predictive analytics, forecasting, and business intelligence. Eg: DataRobot, Alteryx.
- **Synthetic Data Generation** : Creating artificial datasets for AI model training, especially in scenarios where real-world data is scarce, sensitive, or costly to obtain. Eg: Mostly AI, Gretel.ai.
- **AI Ethics and Compliance Tools** : Developing frameworks and tools for ensuring ethical AI use, adherence to regulations, and mitigating biases in AI systems. Eg: Parity AI, Fairly AI.

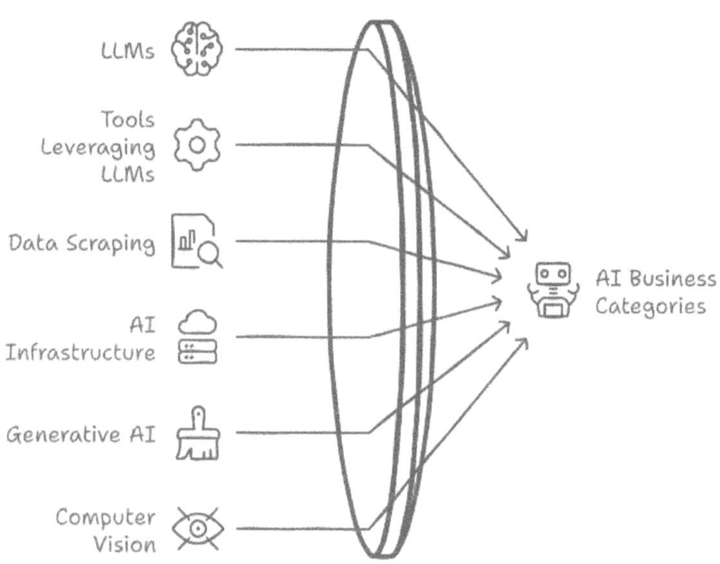

Technology Focussed AI Business

Summary

Chapter 1 - Introduction

The chapter introduces the transformative journey of Artificial Intelligence (AI) from a speculative concept to an indispensable technology shaping modern life. Highlighting AI's evolution from the mid-20th century, it covers pivotal milestones, including early theoretical ideas from visionaries like Alan Turing and John McCarthy, through periods of both growth and stagnation, such as the "AI Winters." Also, emphasizes breakthrough innovations like IBM's Deep Blue and AlphaGo, which demonstrated AI's capability to surpass human expertise in complex games. The chapter concludes by showcasing how AI became deeply integrated into daily life with tools like Siri, Alexa, and ChatGPT, reflecting its ongoing evolution and the significant role it plays across industries and personal interactions.

Chapter 2 - 1950s: Computer Technology

In the 1950s, computers marked the dawn of digital computing, occupying entire rooms and powered by vacuum tubes and magnetic drums. These machines relied on punch cards for data input and performed basic arithmetic and logical tasks, which were groundbreaking at the time. Early programming was done in machine and assembly languages, with FORTRAN emerging later in the decade for scientific applications. Despite their limitations, 1950s computers laid the foundational architecture, processing capabilities, and problem-solving focus that set the stage for today's advanced AI and computing technologies.

Chapter 3 - 1950-1960: Alan Turing And World War II

This chapter explores Alan Turing's transformative contributions to computing and cryptography during a pivotal era. At Bletchley Park, he played a crucial role in cracking the Enigma code, an encryption system used by Nazi Germany, and developed the Bombe machine, which significantly improved the speed and accuracy of deciphering German messages. His efforts not only helped shorten World War II but also laid the groundwork for modern computing. After the war, Turing introduced the Turing Test to evaluate machine intelligence and proposed the Universal Turing Machine, a concept foundational to computer science. His groundbreaking ideas on programming, problem-solving, and machine intelligence continue to influence advancements in AI and computational thinking.

Chapter 4 - Inside 1950 Computer Technology

In the summer of 1956, the Dartmouth Conference marked the official beginning of artificial intelligence as a formal field of study. A small group of visionary scientists, led by John McCarthy, Marvin Minsky, Nathaniel Rochester, and Claude Shannon, gathered at Dartmouth College with a bold goal: to explore the idea that machines could be made to "think." McCarthy coined the term "Artificial Intelligence" to capture this vision of creating machines that could replicate human intelligence through reasoning, perception, and language. The conference attendees aimed to push the boundaries of computer science by combining mathematics, engineering, psychology, and logic to simulate human thought processes. Though the immediate outcome was theoretical, the attendees went on to make critical innovations, such as developing the LISP programming language and founding the MIT AI Lab and more, which became pivotal in shaping the AI field.

Chapter 5 - 1970s: The First AI Winter

The 1970s marked the first "AI Winter," a period of stagnation in artificial intelligence research and development. Optimism from earlier breakthroughs gave way to challenges such as technical limitations, including slow and expensive hardware and a lack of computational power. Overpromised goals by researchers led to public skepticism when advancements failed to meet expectations. Competition from other fields like software engineering further drew resources away from AI. This decline led to reduced funding, scaled-back research, and a negative perception of AI's potential. Despite the setbacks, this era provided valuable lessons, redirecting efforts toward more realistic, task-specific applications, eventually fueling the revival of AI in later decades.

Chapter 6 - 1980s: The Rise Of Expert Systems

The 1980s marked a revival of AI through the emergence of expert systems, which simulated human decision-making in specialized fields. These expert systems utilized rule-based logic, inference engines, and knowledge bases to solve complex problems in domains such as healthcare, chemistry, and geology. Notable examples include DENDRAL, which assisted chemists; CATS, which supported aircraft maintenance; MYCIN, which aided in diagnosing bacterial infections; and PROSPECTOR, which identified valuable mineral deposits. Expert systems were mostly written in LISP and Prolog and typically ran on mainframes and advanced workstations, with some systems like XCON achieving significant commercial success. They also drove the adoption of programming languages like LISP and Prolog, essential for symbolic reasoning. However, their reliance on extensive human effort for maintenance made them expensive and difficult to sustain, ultimately paving the way for more adaptable AI technologies in the near future.

Chapter 7 - 1986: The Introduction Of Neural Networks

The 1986 revival of neural networks marked a turning point in AI, fueled by the introduction of backpropagation, an algorithm redefined by Geoffrey Hinton, David Rumelhart, and Ronald Williams. Inspired by the human brain, neural networks like the Multilayer Perceptron (MLP) leveraged backpropagation to correct errors and improve learning. This innovation allowed networks to process complex data and adapt effectively. Applications included handwriting recognition, image classification, and speech recognition, demonstrating neural networks' ability to solve intricate pattern-recognition tasks. The era also emphasized data-driven AI, highlighting the importance of feeding large datasets for better learning. These breakthroughs laid the groundwork for modern machine learning, establishing neural networks as a cornerstone in AI's evolution and setting the stage for deep learning advancements.

Chapter 8 - 1986 - 1995: The Second AI Winter

The Second AI Winter (1987–1995) reflected diminishing confidence in AI's ability to meet its promises. Despite optimism from the success of expert systems, AI projects faced challenges like limited processing power and constrained memory. Events such as the collapse of the Lisp machine market, reduced funding from defense agencies, and commercial struggles in finance highlighted the growing disillusionment. The decline of interest in expert systems and the failure of Japan's Fifth Generation Computer Systems project further exemplified the technological and financial limitations of the time. However, this period also emphasized realistic goals and laid the groundwork for modern AI by focusing on scalable, data-driven models, marking a shift towards machine learning and pragmatic AI advancements.

Chapter 9 - 1997: Super Computer Defeats A Chess Grandmaster

In 1997, IBM's Deep Blue achieved a groundbreaking milestone in artificial intelligence by defeating Garry Kasparov, the reigning chess world champion, in a six-game rematch under standard tournament rules. This victory marked the first time a computer triumphed over a world champion in a full match, showcasing AI's potential to rival human cognitive abilities in complex strategic tasks. Deep Blue's development journey spanned years of refinement, integrating advanced algorithms, evaluation functions, and the capacity to process millions of chess positions per second. This achievement captured global media attention, sparking debates on AI's broader implications and establishing AI as a serious field of innovation. The event highlighted AI's potential, setting the stage for advancements in machine learning and data-driven technologies.

Chapter 10 - 2000s: Machine Learning And The Rise Of Data

The 2000s marked a transformative era for AI, driven by the rise of machine learning and the explosion of digital data. With the widespread adoption of the internet, smartphones, and connected devices, massive datasets became available, fueling the growth of ML algorithms. Techniques like supervised, unsupervised, and reinforcement learning enabled systems to learn from data, uncover patterns, and make predictions, revolutionizing industries like healthcare, finance, and retail. Key algorithms, including decision trees, SVMs, and neural networks, laid the groundwork, while infrastructure such as GPUs, HPC, and tools like Hadoop supported scalability. Despite challenges like computational limits, data privacy, and bias, this era established the foundation for deep learning, advancing AI from research to impactful real-world applications and reshaping the future of technology.

Chapter 11 - 2010s: The Rise Of Deep Learning

The 2010s marked a transformative era in artificial intelligence with the rise of deep learning, inspired by the human brain's neural networks. This approach used layered artificial neurons to analyze, identify patterns, and make decisions from vast datasets. Deep learning's success was fueled by advancements in computational power, particularly GPUs and TPUs, and access to massive datasets. It surpassed traditional machine learning in handling unstructured data like images, speech, and natural language. Deep learning revolutionized industries, enabling breakthroughs in medical imaging, autonomous vehicles, personalized recommendations, fraud detection, and virtual assistants like Siri. Despite challenges like interpretability and computational intensity, deep learning brought AI closer to human-like understanding, reshaping industries and laying the groundwork for future innovations.

Chapter 12 - 2010s: The Rise Of Natural Language Processing (NLP)

The 2010s marked a transformative decade for NLP, propelled by deep learning advancements. NLP evolved from simple rule-based systems to sophisticated neural networks capable of understanding context, tone, and meaning in human language. This era witnessed an explosion of unstructured text data, driven by social media and digital communications, which necessitated advanced NLP technologies for interpreting and analyzing language. Python and Java emerged as key tools for building NLP models, while frameworks like NLTK and spaCy facilitated tasks like sentiment analysis, topic modeling, and text classification. Real-world applications spanned email spam detection, and social media sentiment analysis. By bridging the gap between human communication and machine understanding, NLP reshaped industries, enabling seamless human-machine interactions.

Chapter 13 - 2010 - 2022: Tech Gaints Driving Innovation

The 2010–2022 era highlighted AI's transformative power, led by tech giants like Google, Microsoft, IBM, Amazon, and Apple. These companies revolutionized industries by advancing AI-driven solutions in machine learning, natural language processing, and cloud-based applications. Innovations like Google's TensorFlow and Microsoft's Cognitive Services democratized AI tools, while IBM's Watson brought AI into healthcare, retail, and finance. Apple's Siri and Face ID redefined user-device interaction. Cloud computing facilitated AI scalability, enabling breakthroughs in autonomous driving, fraud detection, and personalized recommendations. Each company's contributions not only shaped their respective industries but also set the stage for the future of AI. This period solidified AI as a central force in technological innovation, impacting billions of lives globally.

Chapter 14 - 2010 - 2022: AI Startups Revolution

This chapter explores the transformative impact of AI startups from 2010 to 2022, highlighting their pivotal role in advancing artificial intelligence. These startups innovated in areas like generative AI, data annotation, and content creation, pushing the boundaries of AI's capabilities. Companies such as OpenAI, DeepMind, and Scale AI revolutionized industries through groundbreaking tools and technologies, while collaborations and acquisitions by tech giants amplified their influence. By addressing challenges like scalability and efficiency, these startups reshaped domains from healthcare to autonomous systems. Their agility and vision not only redefined the AI landscape but also laid the foundation for future innovations, marking a significant period in the evolution of artificial intelligence.

Chapter 15 - 2010 - 2022: The Unnoticed AI

The chapter highlights how artificial intelligence seamlessly integrated into daily life. Initially confined to back-end systems and industry applications, AI began enhancing user experiences through voice assistants like Siri and Alexa, personalized recommendations on streaming platforms, and social media optimization. AI also improved efficiency in healthcare diagnostics, financial fraud detection, agriculture, and education. It played a crucial role in smart homes, autonomous vehicles, and space exploration by leveraging technologies like machine learning and natural language processing. By tailoring content, automating tasks, and improving decision-making, AI quietly transformed multiple sectors. The chapter emphasizes AI's ability to adapt to human needs, making advanced technology an unnoticed yet indispensable part of modern life.

Chapter 16 - 2022: The Rise Of ChatGPT And LLM's

The chapter highlights the transformative rise of ChatGPT and Large Language Models (LLMs) in 2022, marking a new era in AI-driven human-computer interaction. Powered by transformer-based architectures, LLMs like GPT-3 excel in understanding and generating human-like language. ChatGPT's launch by OpenAI showcased the ability of these models to engage in contextual conversations, adapt to user input, and provide intuitive assistance. Challenges such as bias, misinformation, and resource demands are acknowledged, yet LLMs have revolutionized fields like education, business, and daily life. By redefining digital communication with personalized, adaptive responses, ChatGPT exemplifies the potential of AI to bridge human and machine interactions. This evolution fuels innovation, setting the stage for intelligent, conversational systems that reshape technology's role in society.

Conclusion

Over the past 72 years, AI has evolved from a pioneering concept in 1950 to a vital part of our lives. From its roots in academic research to its integration into countless applications, AI has gradually become integral to modern society, especially over the last decade. Today, it powers advancements in healthcare, streaming, social media, public safety, and more, reflecting its profound impact on daily life.

As of 2024, AI has become mainstream, transforming industries and sparking new innovations in fields like generative AI, where machines can create images, videos, music, and text. AI agents and automation tools are reshaping workflows and boosting creativity. However, as AI's influence grows, so does the need for laws and governance, leading to the rise of AI-based regulations and ethical guidelines worldwide. Countries and organizations are working to address privacy, bias, and accountability, ensuring responsible AI use and protecting public interests.

This journey of AI, from theoretical exploration to a central role in technology, highlights both its incredible potential and the responsibility it carries. The rapid advancement of AI continues to redefine possibilities, offering tools that bridge human creativity with machine intelligence. As we look to the future, AI promises to enhance our lives further, supported by evolving laws that guide its ethical and responsible integration into society.

Author Note

Thank you for embarking on this journey through the pages of this book. I hope it has offered you both an enjoyable experience and a deeper understanding of the fascinating history of artificial intelligence. My aim has been to share the evolution of AI and its remarkable milestones, from its conceptual beginnings to its impactful role in our lives today.

Through each chapter, we've seen how AI has developed not only as a technological force but also as a tool that shapes industries, assists in daily tasks, and opens new frontiers for human potential. With AI continuing to grow, the journey of learning and discovery has only just begun. Thank you again for taking the time to explore AI's rich history with me, I look forward to the innovations that await us all in the future.

With gratitude..!!

Mohammed Yousef Shaik
AI Entrepreneur and Innovator - Business, Creativity, and Knowledge

Chennai - India - 2024